Whyology

Understanding Why We Do What We Do

TJ Jomha LL.B.

For requests about this work please write to:

Whyology at #1050, 10020 – 101A Avenue, Edmonton, Alberta, Canada, T5J 3G2

ISBN: 1482516446
ISBN-13: 978-1482516449

DEDICATION

This book is dedicated to: my brothers, my mother and father, the whole Jomha family, the boys, the girls, my friends who listened to me talk about this project for eight years, and my editors—Mark Kozub and Barbara North.

I also dedicate this book to: Dr. D. Wardell, Dr. Marcia Spetch, Dr. F. Epling, Dr. B.F. Skinner, Dr. Ivan Pavlov, Thomas Hobbes, Aristotle, Dr. Sigmund Freud, my clients, my colleagues, the University of Alberta, the Province of Alberta, the City of Edmonton and last, but certainly not least, the great Country of Canada for allowing my father here in 1957 with 20 dollars in his pocket and allowing me the ability to get to this point.

Certain names in the text of this book are fictitious in order to protect their identities

CONTENTS

CHAPTER 1 - The Enlightenment

This book will change the way you look at people and the world forever. It will change the way you see the behavior of others and alter the way you behave toward them. It will shed light on actions and processes you didn't really think about before, and you will see more deeply into everything around you, into the universal activity that is always humming away. You will see yourself reflected in the behavior of others of all ages and across all walks of life, and you will begin to manipulate your actions so that your world is more in tune with your needs and your resounding self-interest. This book will help you to understand those around you and assist you in all dealings with others, whether for business or for pleasure. Read this book with caution and read it carefully.

I wrote this book for a casual observer, and I include many examples of how psychological principles work in everyday life. I wrote it in layman's terms and made it as palatable as possible, without sacrificing some of the complex language, so that it would impact and be understood by a vast audience. I want to answer your questions about why people do the things they do in the world in which we live. I want to magnify the universal laws of human behavior that connect us via a common thread. By uncovering the laws of behavior, you can alter your behavior to make your life more fulfilling.

Understanding the world around us means looking closely at the small components that make up that world. This means training the eye to see all the tiny little pieces of action, reaction, biology, and society that make up the seemingly unified people we want to be and live with. My aim is for you, the reader, to take away certain principles and concepts that will help you understand this world, and the ways in which you act in it and shape it for your betterment. For those of you in doubt, you can verify a lot of the things you are about to read for yourself in everyday life, just by sitting and observing the unfettered natural behaviors of people in their everyday world.

Writing this book was very difficult because I needed to properly frame what I meant or the book would not be truly effective. Some may be puzzled, some may be confused, but think long and hard, always be observant, and it will all fall into place. Writing this book was analogous to carving an intricate sculpture. It took me countless hours of revision, editing, and fine tuning until it took the shape laid out before you.

I was born in Edmonton, Alberta, Canada and grew up in a family of five boys. My eldest brother completed two degrees (business and science) at the University of Alberta. My second oldest brother completed his science and dental degrees. My second youngest brother graduated with a law degree. My youngest brother went into business with my father at the age of 14 and has since been lighting up sales. We can probably say that my brothers and I came from good genetic stock. I'm the middle son of the five boys, which can be a challenging place to be at times.

My father arrived by boat on the east coast of Canada in 1957. He traveled around Canada until he settled in Edmonton, where the Jomha family had roots dating back to the 1880s. Upon settling here, my father worked odd jobs such as packing boxes for 75 cents an hour. He also attended night school to learn basic English so that he could get ahead. In 1959 he went into the shoe business with his brother and has been doing that ever since. My mother worked tirelessly day and night as a housewife feeding her six males like a pride of hungry lions. My parents gave us life and worked hard for us, and it is because of their efforts, that I have been able to enjoy the unlimited opportunity that they and Canada have afforded me. I am forever grateful to them and to Canada.

From a young age I was always curious about why adults behaved in the ways they did. I was always a people watcher, examining all of their moves and wondering *why*. Why do we do the things we do? It wasn't until a couple of years into university that I truly realized just how deeply I wanted to know the things that propelled our behavior in a multitude of directions. It was then that it all began to unravel. There was a treasure chest in my head just waiting to be opened. It was that constant pursuit about the truth of human behavior that brought me to this point.

After I completed high school, I had to follow in my eldest brothers' footsteps and go to university. I was both terrified and excited of going to university. This was the cream of the academic crop, and I would have to lay it all out to be competitive. At the time, the University of Alberta graded on a nine-point system as opposed to the more common four-point system. The grading scale went from one to nine: A student needed at least a four to pass a class, and a nine was the top mark anyone could receive in a class. The nines were attained by about the top 3 % of the class and sometimes even as little as the top 1% of the class. To put it into perspective, in a class of 200 people, there would be only two to six nines attainable, depending on how many the professor decided to award. They have since changed to a four-point system to fall more in line with other North American institutions.

The grading system in many of my classes was based on a standard bell curve. The curve of the line in a bell shape is where people fall on a graph, with most people bunched up in the middle, making the average. You then have a skinny end on each side: one for the "wizards" at the right end, and one for the "flops" who forgot there was an exam that day on the left (more likely a combination of disadvantageous genes and a poor environment). For those of you out there not familiar with a bell curve, here is an example. Let's say that if you got 60% on an exam, and the class average was 40%, you would likely get a nine (depending on the standard deviation). This would be the highest mark attainable because you'd be at the right end of the bell curve, which was well above the average of the class.

In my first year at the University of Alberta, I was enrolled in the Faculty of Science, majoring in chemistry. I didn't mind the classes, but I just hated the chemistry labs. They were endlessly long, and I would come out of them smelling like sulphur and other nasty chemicals. It wasn't until my third year of university that I realized that I had a natural talent for understanding psychology. I was very proficient in the field of behavioral psychology. I discovered it by accident—yes, by serendipity: I was extremely and surprisingly bright when it came to behavioral psychology, without ever knowing it beforehand. It just came to me like one plus one. I didn't know how or *why*, it just did.

It was that accidental discovery that brings me here. It is like the accidental discovery of penicillin. It wasn't planned; it just interrupted the expected course of my life. It was just one of those things lying just beneath the surface waiting to be unearthed, and I didn't realize it until I was 20 years old. This was the enlightenment period for me. It was uncovering a hidden treasure that I didn't know I had until my mind began to open. This was my true passion, my inherited gift.

All these years I had a hidden talent wired into my mental hardware. I just never had the means of finding out about it because I never encountered the right conditions that could test it or summon it from deep within my psyche. At last, I had found an institution that would test my mind and be the catalyst to unlock the sleeping brilliance inside of me. The university inspired and exposed me to a branch of science I was ready to master. My mind began to open as I learned more about behavioral psychology. I really began to hone my skills in the subject. My natural intellectual gifts became coupled with a continual curiosity for observing people's behavior in their everyday environment.

My period of enlightenment began when I registered in Psychology 104, *Basic Psychology*, in my second year of university. It was just a general psychology course that I thought would be interesting. I had my first midterm about a month into the class. I think I got about 70% on that first exam, which on the nine point scale was good for about a six, or class average. I was not too happy about that, but I moved on.

The middle portion of the course was in behavioral psychology, and so was my next psychology exam. I scored very well on the exam, even surprising myself. I thought that I had fluked out on the second exam, although I remember that the answers seemed to almost jump out at me. However, I just thought this was from thorough studying. The last exam in the class, the final, didn't go as well, and I finished the class with a seven. It was above average—good, but not good enough.

In my third year, I enrolled in Psychology 281, *Principles in Behavior*, a full course in behavioral psychology. I wrote the first midterm and did extremely well on it. The day we got our marks back I was sitting in my living room at home with a bad cold, and my cousin called me from school. He was in my class and told me that I got one of the top marks in the class. This was back in the day when the internet was in its infancy and they still posted marks up on the walls. I was happy to hear that I scored well, especially due to the fact that there were 261 people enrolled in the class. I ended up finishing the class with a nine. I believe only one other person attained a grade of nine in that class. So, less than one percent of the class received a grade of nine, and I was one of them. I was overjoyed when I received my final grade.

It became apparent to me as I was in Psychology 281 that the second midterm that I had written in Psychology 104 and scored well on was no fluke at all. For some reason I knew the stuff better than I should have. I had an uncanny talent for understanding behavioral psychology far better than average. For some odd reason this branch of psychology was second nature to me. I understood it more in depth than I even knew at the time. However, I needed more testing to be convinced of my sheer brilliance in the discipline.

The next semester I enrolled in Psychology 271, *Personality*, which was tied to behavioral and other models of psychology. There were 238 people enrolled in that class. A classmate told me the final grades were posted in the biological sciences building, and I was eager to check my grade. I distinctly remember walking up to the building and repeating to myself, "Please give me an eight, please give me an eight," as I needed it to keep my grade point average up. I was astonished that I had attained a grade of nine in the class. The subject matter in the course was tied to what I had been doing in Psychology 281. It was in Psychology 271 that I really began to think of the behavior of humans at a much deeper level. I started to observe the people around me more and more and became really in tune with what made people tick. I continued as I had always done, observing people's moment to moment behavior at a deep level of understanding, now using a theoretical framework based on academic knowledge.

It was while studying for a Psychology 271 exam late one night in the library that I told myself that I would write about this subject when I was finished school. I found I had a powerful knowledge of the area, and this would surely contribute something to society. After reading the ideas of Freud, Jung, Maslow, Skinner, Pavlov, Descartes, Aristotle and others, I became immersed, and somewhat obsessed, in the pursuit of the laws that governed human behavior. I would attempt to crack the code and deliver my theory and insights of human behavior to the world.

The best way to assess and explain behavioral psychology is to observe it in a multitude of contexts. Behavior is not readily measurable by some instrument or unit: it is what it is. That is why you will have to validate what I say in this book for yourself and come to your own conclusions. That is the best way to understand and envision for yourself exactly what this is all about. I'm certain many who read this book will do just that. *Why?* Because I feel so passionately about what I am writing about, and because I believe in it so much, I feel it necessary to present the world this knowledge for better or for worse. I want you to have those "a-ha!" moments just as I did after being in certain situations and when interacting with others.

My mental engine for behavioral psychology was really getting warm now, and I was at the brink of realizing just how deeply and comprehensively I understood the discipline. In my fourth year of university I enrolled in Psychology 381, *Principles of Learning*, another behavioral psychology course. I remember a week after the first midterm, our professor said that our marks were posted up in the science building. Just before the class was over, I slipped out to be the first to see my mark, as I knew there would be a crowd right after class around where the marks were posted. Apparently, a lot of other students followed, and I had a herd of students behind me as I approached the board where the marks were posted by I.D. number.

I walked up to the board, which was littered with papers stapled to it showing different class lists of marks. I felt those light butterflies in my stomach that you get before you are about look at a grade for an exam you wrote. I wasn't too nervous because I thought I had done well anyway. I found my I.D. number and put my finger on it with many onlookers behind me. I slowly slid my finger across the sheet from my I.D. number to where my grade was. I could feel all of the eyes behind me watching as my index finger slowly neared my grade. I stopped at my grade with my fingernail dug on the page just below it. Those butterflies in my stomach turned back into caterpillars as I swallowed abruptly. I aced it. Yes, that's right: one hundred percent. I was elated. I turned around, and seeing all of my classmates' eyes on me, I couldn't help notice how green they all were with envy. I remember seeing some other grades, and noticed that some people even failed. *Who were those morons?* I thought.

I proudly walked away from the scene. It was like a scene out of the movie *Good Will Hunting* and at that very moment I knew I was on to something big. I ended up finishing the class with a nine, of course, because this stuff was so elementary to me. It was like finger painting. I even missed a film shown in class about gorilla behavior and still got those questions right on the exam. I knew this stuff on an entirely different level than the rest of the "kids."

The next semester I enrolled in Psychology 385, *Behavioral Therapy and the Applications of Learning*, which investigated methods of behavioral psychology in the treatment of people with certain phobias and other psychopathologies (mental disorders and/or behavioral issues). I bet you can guess what I got in that class. Yes, another nine. I achieved the top grade in a class of 127 people, many of whom were psychology majors.

I distinctly remember a question I got wrong on the first midterm exam in Psychology 385. The question was: "Which of the following is a continuous positive reinforcer?" A continuous positive reinforcer is something of benefit or value to you that you receive after you commit a certain behavior, which makes that behavior more likely to occur in the future. It will constantly be rewarding, no matter how many times you get it. The choices were: (a) food, (b) money, (c) social praise, or (d) all of the above. I knew that it wasn't food, because people get full from food and it loses it reinforcing value/effect after a while. I knew it wasn't (d), all of the above, because if (a) wasn't right, (d) couldn't be right.

So I was left with two answers that I knew were both correct. How could this be? If there were two right answers, and I only had a choice of one, I had a fifty-fifty chance of getting it right. Was my excellence in psychology being questioned here? What could it be? Maybe the professor forgot to write a fifth answer: "(e) (b) and (c)." I chose social praise. I realized I got the question wrong after getting my exam back (although I should mention I believe I got the highest mark in the class).

I remember walking up to the professor at the break and saying "Excuse me, Sir, but I have an issue with one of the questions on your exam." He replied, "Oh yeah, which one?" I proceeded to show him that both money and social praise could serve as continuous positive reinforcers. I explained to him that after Wayne Gretzky scores a goal and the fans cheer, that is social praise. Even if the effects of that become diminished after a period of continuous reinforcement, there is still some reinforcing value from the social praise. Similarly, there would still be some reinforcing value if a billionaire received $50,000 for doing something. As slight as the reinforcing value may be, it is reinforcing nonetheless, so it is a continuous positive reinforcer. Just because the saliency of the reinforcing effect may sometimes be higher for money, it still does not negate the fact that social praise is a continuous reinforcer.

The professor disagreed with me and asked what I got on the exam. When I told him my grade, he freaked out and said "give me a break." What he didn't understand is that it wasn't about the 1% (the exam was 100 questions, each worth 1%), it was the fact that there were two correct answers and I was right. It was about the science to me, not the grade. I had a nine after the exam anyway, so one more mark didn't matter. He didn't like the fact that I questioned his answers, and he told me not to worry about it. I walked away feeling a little ripped off and a little dejected because I knew I was right, and he wouldn't give credit where credit was due.

I was now at the apex of my grasp of behavioral psychology. I would say that it was right around this time that I began to think I was a mastermind in this area of science. I know it sounds a bit conceited, but, what the hell—I had proved my abilities over and over. Okay, maybe I was getting a little too cocky. I moved on. Well, sort of. I minored in sociology in order to complement my studies in psychology.

I did well in sociology, too, scoring eights in a lot of the classes. However, there was nothing I knew like the content of behavioral psychology, more specifically, the principles of learning and behavior, as well as behavioral modification and manipulation. Other related classes I enrolled in included developmental biology, pharmacology, abnormal psychology, social psychology, and micro and macroeconomics. While in the Faculty of Science, I applied to law school and was accepted. I graduated with a law degree in 2004, yet I still had my mental compass pointed in the direction of behavioral psychology.

I decided to pursue law because I was somewhat materialistic, and I knew I could make a good living after completing my degree. Like many, my true passion was put aside for a well-paying job and all of the things I wanted to have as a student.

There is an old adage, *write what you know*, and here I am. If you have something to say to the world, then say it. If there is one thing I know well, and that I am very talented at, it is behavioral psychology. I don't know why, I just am. It is my true passion. It burns in me and screams in my head, wanting to come out.

9

Just like me, with my affinity for psychology, certain people show the effects of coupling advantageous genes with passion and the proper environment. This affords them the opportunity to become very talented at something, whether it's science or music.

Axl Rose, the lead singer of the rock group Guns N' Roses, wrote the song "Sweet Child of Mine" about Erin Everly, his girlfriend at the time. That song was so successful because it came from deep within him. It was about true meaning: he dug deep, and the product was so sweet (no pun intended). That song was created in him by forces at work that commingled his genetic soup with his environmental experiences. The song is topped off by an amazing guitar solo from Slash. It is a rock masterpiece, a combination of two amazing performers at the apex of their talent and genre. They both dug deep and made it real. The song was in them, and they summoned their talent and channeled it for all to hear. It was what they knew and knew well. So remember: write what you know, or do what you know, and if you have something to say then say it, and say it loud. That's why I'm here. I have something to say about a subject I am very talented at and passionate about.

Once you have read this book, you will never again ask "*Why* would somebody do that?" There is *always* an answer to why people behave the way they do. Fundamentally, people are rational beings who do things for reasons. Every single behavior has an explanation—no matter how erratic, insignificant, banal, or unexpected. Every single action and verbal utterance can be traced back or deduced to *why* a behavior was committed by the actor. It is a simple premise, with so many complicating factors.

Every single thing you do or say has purpose. We are all purposive creatures and all behavior is committed to achieve a purpose, whatever that may be. *All behavior is lawful.* We are *all* rough economists, always weighing the costs and benefits of every single voluntary behavior we do. When the costs and benefits are close in weight, we can be swayed by outer influences, tipping the balance to one decision versus another.

When the costs outweigh the benefits and vice versa, we behave one way as opposed to another. Why? Because we are all mechanisms of pure self-interest from the day we are born until the day we die. I'm not espousing that we are innately good or bad. I'm saying that we are all value seekers, but the reasons and the means lie within each of us and where we find ourselves. What you value depends on your genes and historical context.

Those who want change must help to bring about change within themselves. What I can do is help you to see where the space for change lies, and how even the smallest behaviors can be a part of that change. It is kind of like having a nuclear reactor. Nuclear science is a natural process, cracked open and harnessed by human hands. It can be useful and productive, or dangerous and destructive, depending on how and why people use it.

In the same way, people may use psychology in everyday life for good or for evil. Psychology has been used for centuries for mass manipulation, unscrupulous profiteering, confusing misrepresentation, and worse. However, the goal of this book is to expose the psychological mechanisms at play that cause us to behave the way we do, and to isolate and understand those behavioral principles in better detail so that we can better understand our world and assist those in need.

We can become self-aware actors, able to change behavioral patterns that are harmful to us and to help those around us. We can also bring some tolerance into the world. No person is flawless or without his or her own patterns of harmful behavior. However, maybe knowing what you do and why will make you stronger in kicking off the things that are causing you or others hardship. We must learn and understand the critical elements that drive our behavior if we are seeking to attempt to alter it. That is what *Whyology* is all about: understanding human behavior for future progress and assistance to you and others, ultimately for the benefit of the common good.

The chapters that follow break ordinary action and response into readily graspable principles, making the behavior of people more transparent to those who are in tune with the principles of human behavior and the psychology of everyday life. This book will help you throughout the rest of your life. It will engage and enlighten you. It will give you an edge in everyday life by allowing you to see the angles of people's behavior more clearly and it will teach you to manipulate people and the environment, for better or for worse. This book will prevent you from being manipulated. It will broaden your horizons, and it will make you smarter. Most of all, and the reason I wrote this book, *Whyology* will inspire real thought and dialogue and assist those who are in need of psychological intervention.

11

As a practicing lawyer, understanding the principles of human behavior has helped me immensely with my clients. I am better equipped to handle clients and their needs in numerous ways. This translates into better interpersonal relationships by understanding another person's angles and reacting in accordance to what I think would be more favorable to them. This is of great importance to my business dealings and client satisfaction.

Through observing the behavior of people, I walk around daily validating my theory over and over again. My theory tells me what a person might do next or *why* somebody said or did something. My friends, brothers, nieces, nephews and perfect strangers are all my test subjects and they don't even know they are part of a quasi-experiment. I test my theory daily, using it on people when they don't even know what I am up to. I deliberately do and say things to some people as field experiments: I am interacting with the real world, seeking to validate my theory by eliciting certain responses from people. After observing long enough, I can almost predict what a person will do next. Biobehaviorism, my theory of the behavior of people in their everyday lives, in their everyday world, is what governs our behavior every second of the day, no matter where we are or what we are doing. It applies to all humans regardless of personality or place.

This book applies to you if you are a human being—that is the only prerequisite for needing to read on any further. I will share my careful observations of the world with you, and after carrying on with the daily things in your life in your own idiosyncratic way, these principles will start to make real sense. You, too, will have that scientist who is embedded deep within your mind leap out as you realize what makes people do the things they do. You can validate for yourself that what I lay out here is nothing but the truth. I know it is because I have tested it countless times. Science is about observation, understanding and prediction. It is those observations that lead to theories. I challenge you to test my theory and validate it for yourself. I want you to test it so many times that it becomes a law in your mind. Enter a realm of viewing the world in a different light.

I urge you to pay close attention to what is going on in the world around you and remember some key principles of action and reaction. Once you have truly understood the message of this book, then you may start to manipulate your environment for your own benefit and make more sense of your life. You will start seeing the motivations behind people's behavior, which may assist you in shaping your life and maybe even assist you in drawing those that you love away from dangerous vices, such as gambling or drugs.

If I can leave you with one thing it is that this book will undoubtedly change the way you see people and the social world that you encounter.

CHAPTER 2 - The Everyday Scientist

Let's say that you called your handy Uncle Bill over to your house to do a minor plumbing job, and you tried to pay him $60 for the work he completed. Of course he was offended and didn't take the money. Isn't that a breakdown of my theory of self-interest? Shouldn't Uncle Bill be interested in compensation for his work? That depends on Uncle Bill's value hierarchy. Here, it may be more valuable to Uncle Bill *not* to take the money for reasons only he may know. These reasons could range from Uncle Bill not wanting to seem cheap for not helping the family freely, to discomfort around money. Maybe Uncle Bill places more value on calling in a mysterious favor one day in the future. Maybe he needs something from you. Maybe Uncle Bill knows he did a shoddy job. Whatever the reason, the costs of taking your money may be greater to Uncle Bill than the $60, so he may refuse the money.

Let's scale this up: imagine Uncle Bill does a complete renovation job and he is owed $22,000 for the work. Do you think he will take the money now? You must be thinking, "YES, of course!" The answer is that he might, but I can't say for sure because I don't know how valuable it is for Bill *not* to take the money, regardless of the sum. What we need is some context, but chances are most likely that Uncle Bill would take the payment. However, we can still never be 100% certain until we have more information. Understanding the behavior of others rests on understanding the contextual frame in which they operate and where they have been in their journey through life. Context always matters—whether the current context or the more important historical context.

Whyology is basically the study of why people commit the behaviors they do. My focus here is on the human subject because of the large brains and complex minds of human beings. The better you understand the crux of the theory of biobehaviorism, the more of a 'whyologist' you will become. The working title for this book was *A Billion Little Pieces* because I began to see life as being divided into roughly a billion segments or frames of time.

I like to think about it like this: The average life expectancy for a person in North America is roughly 80 years. So, if there are 60 seconds in a minute and 60 minutes in an hour, then there are 3,600 seconds in an hour, 86,400 seconds in a day, and 31,536,000 seconds in a year. If we multiply the seconds in a year by the average life expectancy of a person in Canada or the USA, we get 2,522,880,000 seconds that we are alive. Take a third of those seconds off for sleep, and we are left with roughly 1,681,920,000 seconds that we are self-interest seeking organisms. In the average life span of 80 years, it helps us to think of life of being broken up into a billion self-interested segments that are roughly 1.68 seconds in length. Across a lifetime, the average human in North America will commit about a billion different behaviors in a continual struggle to satisfy his or her self-interest.

What governs how we behave can be seen and understood from moment to moment as we are propelled by our drives, fears, beliefs, wishes, desires and needs—all of which are tied to value and genetic undertones. These value-driven mechanisms are continually at work, becoming fine-tuned as they push and pull us in different directions, knocking us against what we encounter in the environment.

Thomas Hobbes laid out a compelling account of self-interest in his political tract *Leviathan*, written in 1651. Hobbes argued that basic life is comprised of the motions of a man going through life as a selfish animal in a constant state of war with all other men. Hobbes spoke on a macro-social level about the condition of men and how they would interact and be at war with one another if it were not for some higher power (governance) keeping all men in check. Hobbes contended that "[h]ereby it is manifest that during the time men live without a common power to keep them all in awe, they are in that condition which is called war; and such a war as is of every man against every man."[1]

Whereas Hobbes spoke of the macro and social consequences of man, I speak of the micro world of behavior and the moment-to-moment processes of human interaction, infusing recent discoveries in genetics for understanding human behavior from the inside out. Hobbes' central premise holds strong: "…of the voluntary acts of every man, the object is some good to himself."[2] I believe, as Hobbes did, that all voluntary human behavior is based on self-interest. However, I look at the actions of man from a purely scientific and psychological standpoint.

The "good" in Hobbes' statement is synonymous with value and interest. There is always self-interest at play, taken as a basic law of voluntary human behavior. However, it remains theory because it cannot be empirically verified, even though I feel that there is a theoretical proof for all of the behavioral actions of mankind. Nevertheless, deducing that proof would be a next to impossible task, and we do not have the capability to do so at this time, though we may be able to formulate it sometime in the future. It's doubtful, though: it might be the unsolvable proof.

Because of our complex genetic make-ups and our vast amounts of worldly experiences, the formula for future behavior would be one of the most complex proofs ever attempted. However, it can loosely be done in theory. The future behavior of man can be predicted with a modest level of precision. I am sure of one thing though: the struggle to satisfy our self-interest occurs every second that we are awake, from the day we are born until the moment we take our last breath.

The precise way this book or tablet is positioned as you read it is a matter of your self-interest. The way your hands are holding it, or the way it sits on a desk, or however else it is situated, is serving your needs in some way that makes sense to you. Your position in relation to this book takes your needs into account: the muscles in your back and neck may be tense from reading in the same position, or you may be angling for the light, or trying to balance a cup of coffee. Now that I alerted you to the way you may be holding this book, I may have made you self-conscious about it. You may have switched positions from the suggestion of it, or maybe you haven't. Maybe your arm is getting tired from being in the same position. Only you know that, and only you know whether the perceived benefits of moving positions into something more comfortable outweigh the perceived costs of the effort, for you are at the center of your every action. You are the rough economist.

Our primary motivation is self-interest, which is inextricably linked to what we have come to value via our drives, fears, beliefs, wishes, desires and needs. It is true that many actions are loosely motivated by fear and hope, but it's not so simple. Every behavior we commit, or word we say, is attributable to something that has value to us, whatever that may be. Buying crack cocaine has real value to an addict, at least in his perception. A person who has no interest in crack wouldn't even pay a penny for it because it has no value to them whatsoever. In fact, for some it is a cost even to be in its vicinity, so it has a negative value—or more aptly and scientifically speaking, it is punishing. To some people, the benefits of smoking cigarettes greatly outweigh the costs. That's why so many people do it. It is through our historical interactions with the environment, as we develop both physically and mentally, that our repertoire of self-interest forms and morphs. This is never exclusive from the genetic vessels (i.e. our bodies) we find ourselves in, for those vessels gauge the value of what we encounter in the real world. We will continue to strive for those value laden targets in our environment after we realize that they have extrinsic or intrinsic value to us.

These properties of value will change over time for all humans, because after all, we are mutable biological creatures at the apex of the animal kingdom, and we are in an ever-evolving world. We cannot discount the fact that our biological clocks morph our self-interest priorities as we all journey through the game of life. Our value systems are fluid and dynamic, built up and altered relative to how we are reinforced (or punished) in our environments. What we value is ultimately determined by us as our genetic manifestations locked in our inherited codes clash with the environment. Our minds are malleable like soft clay, and our beliefs can readily be altered and hardened by experience. It is all about what we perceive as bringing value to ourselves by what value we have attributed to the stimuli in our environment.

I didn't step onto an airplane until the age of 28. I had serious anxiety about flying, even though I always heard the same story about air travel being the safest mode of major transportation for the number of people safely reaching their destination point. I love driving, though. Maybe I'm just a bit of a control freak, and I don't like to know that someone I have never met has my life in his or her hands. Driving gives me the control and response I like.

My friend from university moved to Vancouver because the job prospects for Crime Scene Investigators (CSIs) were good there, and she asked me to fly down to Vancouver and visit her. I thought, *Oh God, what do I do?* How could I tell my friend that I had a fear of flying, even though I had no good reason for it? What would she think of me? I believed I was afraid. I am still afraid, but in January of 2005 I booked a ticket to Vancouver. I wanted my flight to be as comfortable as possible because I was going into anxious territory here. Still, why did I get on that plane even in the face of numbing anxiety? I did so because the perceived benefits outweighed the perceived costs.

The value of seeing my good friend, taking a holiday in a great city like Vancouver, and at the same time experiencing my anxiety head-on was more valuable than avoidance. If I didn't get on that plane, I knew that my relationship with her would be doomed, so I buckled myself in because of self-interest and no other reason. For me, flying came with the perceived costs of intense anxiety and fear attached to the experience. Other costs of never flying included my friends mocking my fear, and restrictions on the places I could visit and the activities I could enjoy. However, those costs were eclipsed by the perceived benefits that I was to reap in performing the act. Thus, I committed the act because the benefits slightly eclipsed the costs. If you want to overcome a fear or phobia of something, using something of high value to conquer that fear is very useful.

It is truly amazing how the people we really value can have an influence on our behavior. It is also amazing how meeting the right girl or guy can totally change someone and allow them to meet their fears head on. Nothing lights a fire under a man like meeting a girl he really likes a lot; cash can't even compete at times. Love and attraction feed a core drive and spur our interest like nothing else.

I come from a large family with an array of personalities. One of my cousins had a problem with gambling. He met a very pretty girl who would have none of it. He quit the vice that had consumed him for years because the cost of losing this girl meant more to him than quitting. Conversely, the benefit of having the girl in his life outweighed the benefits of gambling. So, he stopped when she asked him to, even though he had built up years of attachment to the habit. Sometimes, meeting the right people at the right time can set off a chain of behavioral changes throughout our lives. Scientifically speaking, she was an extreme positive reinforcer because he would get to see her if he wasn't gambling. She had great value to him. We can use extreme positive reinforcers in our own environment to conquer our biggest addictions and phobias. It is this understanding of the costs and benefits that will allow us to make alterations in our lives. We can trump our perceived costly fears or costly behaviors with actions that are more beneficial or valuable and regain control with these positive steps.

I remember watching an interview with Tony Robbins. As a life coach and motivational speaker, Tony Robbins has spoken to many thousands of people on ways in which they can change their lives so as to make their lives more fulfilling. He was asked what group of people were the hardest challenges for him, and he said that it was parents who had lost a child. He said that was one situation in which the parents had a hard time letting go. Losing a child is the ultimate cost to a parent. It is so hard to find a counterweight that could offset the feelings and behaviors related to the loss of a child, and that is *why* these people are the hardest to change. It is because finding something that is more valuable than the life of a child is next to impossible.

Using a very strong positive reinforcer can work directly to overcome fear, addiction or loss unless the fear, addiction or loss is so overwhelming that the reinforcer doesn't have enough value to negate the value one gets from the phobia, addiction or loss. Then the phobia or addiction will fester and go unchecked. It's like my cousin with the bad gambling problem. He loved gambling and loved his girl at the same time. His gambling got so bad that she told him, "You have to make a choice: it's me or the cards." He did some rough economics in his head, because it is all about costs and benefits pitted against one another, as simplistic as that may sound.

I think most guys would quit gambling and choose the girl if they truly loved her. Nevertheless, it still comes down to value in the eyes of the actor. There are some people out there who wouldn't give gambling up for the world because it has attained such great value in their lives that the playing and the rush are better than anything any partner or alternate activity could provide. This holds true for other addictions as well, such as heroin or cocaine. Sometimes the most intrusive intervening events cannot derail the destructive patterns of behavior some people commit, even if they are staring at death or self-capitulation.

Once, I was sitting at the high limit tables in the Palace Casino at West Edmonton Mall talking to a man who was playing blackjack. He looked like a typical gambling degenerate junkie. He had messy hair, cigarette in hand, dirty fingernails, wrinkled clothes, a five o'clock shadow and foul body odor. He was down on his luck and deep into gambling. I was about 20 years old at the time, and he was about 45. He told me to go home and save my money. We kept chatting, and I asked if he was married.

He replied, "Well, my wife told me to make a decision a couple of months back: it was either her and the kids or gambling, and I don't have to tell you which one I chose." He said this as he doubled down a $100 dollar bet and smirked at me. *What a piece of garbage,* I thought. *How on earth could he do that? With kids, too. What a low life.* That was my immediate reaction, but I had to make a conscious effort to understand that there was an explanation as to why he behaved this way. All behavior can readily be explained.

Everything does happen for a reason, and there were reasons that man was gambling and telling me his life story in a nutshell. He lacked the faculties necessary to understand that his behavior was self-destructive and that in the long run the house always wins. Alternatively, he was recklessly blind to it. Even the loss of his family was not a great enough cost to counter the benefit he derived from gambling. This guy was a purveyor of heartache and he didn't have someone to intervene, someone he could have responded to and begun to bring about change.

I shouldn't have been mad, because all human behavior has explanation and can be explained down to the finest and most subtle details. This man was the type of person who I wanted to change: the gambler, the druggie, the addict of any kind, the anorexic, the bulimic, the glutton, the obsessive-compulsive, the hoarder, the phobic, and any others who needed change. This book is for these people.

I was not interested in changing the guy who smokes a joint for fun with his friends or the odd cigarette, for he is not in *need* of change. For something to be problematic in your life, or psychopathological, it must sufficiently interfere with your normal daily life in such a way as to throw you off of your usual routine. For example, many people who use alcohol on a regular basis are routinely late or absent from work. The more intrusive effects the alcohol has on a person's normal routine, the more concerned he or she should be.

We must be careful here using the word "normal." Normal must be looked at along with the context in which "normal" seems to be the norm:

> ...the criteria for determining what behaviors constitute normality may fluctuate according to the dominant economic, social, and political philosophies concurrently operating within any given society.[3]

Nonetheless, where some type of habit, phobia or other psychologically rooted behavior affects someone's pattern of normalcy in his or her given personal and societal framework, he or she is in need of change. As the gap widens between what we consider to be normal and abnormal behavior, so too does the need for intervention. For a person to change, he or she must *want* to change from within.

It is my desire to assist those who leave human suffering in their wake because of destructive drug use or other damaging behavioral patterns. There is so much suffering in this world. It would be a real accomplishment to spare a mother who has had a life of heartache dealing with a son or daughter hooked on some drug or engaged in an otherwise harmful behavior. My goal is to educate the reader by uncovering the mechanisms at play in dangerous behavioral patterns so that readers may curtail and cease such behaviors. For some, a total change of environment may be necessary because context is partly to blame in driving many behavior sequences.

One of the best feelings a person can have is finally kicking an addiction or overcoming a phobia they have been carrying with them for years—like ridding themselves of so much garbage. It is like taking off a pair of ankle shackles that have been weighing on you for your whole life. Take the story of my first plane ride. One way to accomplish change is to graduate away from what it is you need to stop doing or graduate toward something you are afraid of, such as flying. Then you couple this with a strong reinforcer that acts as a counter-reinforcer to your fear or addiction.

Remember, a reinforcer is something that is rewarding in that it either gives the actor something of value or takes something negative away. It is called a reinforcer because it makes the behaviors leading up to that reward more likely to occur in the future. Any stimulus that increases our behavior is reinforcing in that it makes the behavior that led up to that reinforcer more likely to occur in the future. Reinforcers have value, and we are all value chasers.

The problem with the strong reinforcer technique is twofold. Firstly, if the phobia or addiction is so entrenched into someone, there may not be a strong enough counterweight or reinforcer to offset the festering fear or addiction. Secondly, there are some people who have no real passions or reinforcers strong enough to offset whatever the problem behavior is. It is an idiosyncratic approach to achieving an end, but that is

21

how all people must be treated when it comes to the field of psychology. Everyone who has a mental issue, or an addiction, or a phobia must have a treatment regime that is solely tailored to match his or her idiosyncratic needs. This is because, due to genetics and past experiences, we are all different in the pursuit of the self-interest we so crave on a day-to-day basis.

Affection for another can make the most entrenched addicts stop cold turkey, regardless of their addiction, as long as it is of enough value to the actor. Some people are just so far into their pattern of harmful behaviors that even love can't make them stop, because their addiction is so powerful and so gratifying that there is just no substitute to overshadow it. However, the good news is that most patients are treatable. The odd few will slip through the cracks, like the gambling degenerate or the anorexic, and they won't stop until they are broke, dead or physically unable to carry on. For them, nothing can replace the value their destructive behavior gives to them. Nothing can compete with the value of the self-destructing, *yet reinforcing*, behavior.

Even if at first it seems that somebody has done something that doesn't make "economic sense," that is, by examining and comparing the perceived costs and benefits of their actions, only the actor truly knows what's on the tally sheet. Most of the time we can piece together why something was said or done if we are given more of the historical context of people's actions, knowing their beliefs, fears, experiences, values, and so on. When you act as the outside observer, with more information, the whys behind an episode of human action may become clear in your mind. You'll find yourself saying, "Oh, that's why she did that," or, "No wonder he said that. I didn't know about that, but now it all makes sense." It is when you really get to know someone that you learn what pisses them off (or what makes them happy) because you have historical context. You can break their behavior into its components based on what you know about them. It is a deductive task. The better you know someone, the more accurately and easily you can deduce the reasons for their behavior. You will be able to navigate the method of their personal madness based on what you know they value. It is all about value, because we are all value chasers—more specifically, idiosyncratic value chasers, because of our unique genetic codes.

The costs and benefits of things cannot be quantified by some readily available formula. What makes performing an action costly or beneficial depends on how the actor assigns and attributes value to certain things in his or her environment. How things are perceived as costly or beneficial to the actor is determined by a complex mix of the actor's historical interaction with the environment coupled with a person's genetic makeup. Together, these elements underlie biobehaviorism, the theory of action that truly explains all human behavior. It is by clashing with our environment that we determine what is deemed valuable in our physical world through our unique genetic "goggles." This is different for everyone and accounts for our vast cultural and human diversity.

Biobehaviorism represents a constant striving for positive or negative reinforcement (i.e. value) in the environment that is perceived by the actor to have the greatest value, while avoiding costs, all superimposed by the constant variables of genetics. Once again, reinforcing value is determined by our genetic makeup and our past clashes within our environment. It is value that people are after, be it the value they get from helping others, the value they get from dealing drugs, the value they get from working out, the value they get from snorting cocaine, or the value they get by committing suicide. Value is idiosyncratic to the actor. Only they know the costs and benefits. Just how much a person is willing to expend in their struggle for value is in the actor's mind only, based on hard-wired genetic code and previous encounters and exposure with the environment. It's all about value.

Behavior cannot be solely governed by just our genes or just our environment. These two intertwined pieces of the puzzle are constantly working in tandem, shaping and governing our behavior, past, present and future. Our values also change over time by what we perceive as having reinforcing effects in tandem with biological milestones that are programmed into our hardware. This is mainly under the umbrella of genetics because our bodies are programmed to morph in certain ways, such as the physical and mental changes that occur during puberty. These biological milestones shake up our value hierarchies and make us act in different ways as we journey through the game of life.

I strongly assert that the nature-nurture debate is dead. There is no more need for this debate, as it is known that both nature (genetics) and nurture (environmental exposure) govern our lawful, orderly acts. However, I would certainly give more weight to genetic factors. It is these two principles that give value to certain things in the environment and push us in certain directions as we strive to satisfy our self-interest. Tell me what genes your parents passed on to you and where you have been all your life, and I will likely be able to tell you what you will do next or how you will respond in a certain situation.

Different things carry different values to different people. That is why it is hard to predict someone's behavior when you don't really know that person. Knowing people well makes their behavior more predictable for us because we have some conception of their genetic makeup, depending on our relationship to them. We also have some contextual history with those close to us as we see them in their everyday environments. This gives us some insight into determining how they will react to a particular stimulus. If I had the exact genetic makeup of someone, and knew all of their historical interactions with the environment, I could likely predict what someone would do next in a given situation. It would be like plugging values into the elusive mathematical proof of human behavior to get an answer.

Being able to predict someone's actions is highly valuable. I use these concepts in private practice to anticipate what clients want so I can adjust to serve them better. I put them at ease by remaining one step ahead of what they need or of what they are thinking. Parents may also find behavior prediction invaluable in curtailing or preventing unwanted behaviors in their children. Knowing the stimuli that propel behavior can allow us to alter those stimuli so that future occurrences of behavior are more in line with what we seek from ourselves and others.

Human behavior *cannot be* quantified precisely: deducing a proof of human behavior would be one of the most complex things humanity could ever attempt. The proof of human behavior, while *theoretically* plausible, would need more brainpower than possibly all of humanity combined contains. It may be done sometime in the future with some precision via a supercomputer. I believe a rough proof is workable, but it would be so complex and so massive that it would almost lose itself in translation. Theoretically, we could predict behavior with near precision knowing an actor's genetic code and historical context, as these would be variables in the proof of human behavior operating in a vacuum-like state. Even Newton believed that *all* events could be explained, for he believed in the order of events.

The genes that we get from our mothers and fathers are selected randomly in the egg and sperm prior to cell division beginning in the womb. Half of your genetic soup comes from your father and the other half from your mother, as found in the sperm and the egg. Once the sperm meets the egg in the uterus an embryo forms and our genetic code is crystallized. When the egg and sperm meet, a series of molecular events happen to create an embryo. When we exit the womb, predictions can start to be made as we see people interacting in their environment based on the genetic soup they have inherited.

The way people in society collide with one another is like a bunch of atoms orbiting in a fairly predictable path. It is the soup of our genes soaking up our experiences with the environment and strained through our genetic sieves that make our next moves all the more predictable, orderly, and lawful—and all done in the service of self-interest.

How does that affect me? Me me me me me me me me. It is ALL ABOUT YOU, NO MATTER WHAT. Whenever you hear something or someone does something to you, or for you, we always ask the same question. We try to slot whatever we hear or witness into our understanding of the world and the question is always: *How does that affect me?* Why? Because at the core of every action and all behavioral psychology is the self. Let's say you're going to a party, and you expect all your friends to be there. Now you hear that your best friend is skipping out—you're not happy. Why? The party hasn't happened yet, but your understanding of how fun a party will be is based on your previous experience of parties with your best friend. As yet, there has been no behavior to elicit the removal of a positive stimulus, but the information alone has an effect on you due to your preconceived notions of reinforcement. If you didn't have the preconceived notion of your friend being around as a positive inducement to parties, his absence wouldn't matter, but your sense of fun is based on this historical context.

After making my big flight leap, I was contemplating moving to Vancouver for work because I just loved the city when I went down there. I told a friend that I was trying to get an interview with a big law firm in Vancouver. He seemed happy for me, but deep down I knew he wasn't thrilled because his first thought at the news was like it would be for any human: *How does that affect me?* The costs of my leaving were greater than the vicarious benefits to my friend. His discouraging reaction came out of his own preconceived notions of reinforcement. The dilution of our friendship over distance was contrary to his self-interest, regardless of the gains a move might bring to me. To him, my proximate friendship was more valuable than my success.

Some people have argued with me about self-interest by bringing up certain human actions such as volunteering and suicide, as they appear to fly in the face of biobehaviorism. People who volunteer give their time and energy to organizations or issues they are committed to. The personal satisfaction of volunteering and the additional values gained (such as furthering political ends, developing a skill set, or meeting people, etc.) are so rewarding that they trump the costs of time and energy expended without economic (monetary) return. In some way, volunteers perceive their work as a benefit to themselves relative to the costs involved. Helping others helps them feel good about themselves, and it is parallel with their value system.

I had a conversation with a Russian nurse at a party once. Sitting next to her, I didn't have much to say to start off with, so career is always a good ice-breaker. I told her I was a lawyer, and she said, "You must help a lot of people." I replied, "Yeah, sometimes." I asked her about her work and she answered, "I'm a nurse." She began to tell me how selfish she felt she was because she received so much satisfaction from helping others. I stared at her with a new sense of attention. Once again, she buttressed what I thought about the behavior of human beings. Of course she liked nursing: more than money or skill, her choice of occupation was based on her own inclinations. She felt the weight of these selfish interests to the point of actually feeling guilty about getting satisfaction from helping people who were hospitalized.

As I said before, ALL voluntary human behavior is purpose driven and ALL human behavior is lawful, be it voluntary or involuntary. Every moment-to-moment segment of your life, broken up into those tiny little pieces of time, are moments of you striving to get value. It is what you perceive value to be, according to the rough economist you are, as you weigh your historical context, with its costs and benefits. That weighing of perceived costs and benefits makes you act one way or another. Everyone is selfish. They must be. They need to be. Even those who seem to be the most unselfish are still selfish at being unselfish because it makes them feel better. I know it sounds a little strange but it's the truth. People attempt to quell the dissonance within themselves by doing things that they believe will make them feel better.

I read a book entitled *Predictably Irrational* by Dan Ariely.[4] The book attempts to show that people's behavior is irrational and this irrationality can be predictable. As I read the book, I couldn't help thinking to myself that it should be renamed *Unpredictably Rational*, because even though people's decisions seem to be irrational at times, they are in fact rational in their eyes. They are rational because the actor sees them as such and because all behavior is lawful–all decisions are rational in the actors mind and that's what really matters. It is not for outside observers to say that behavior is irrational when the actor sees it as the opposite.

What may be seen as irrational to me may be very rational to another. It's like those who choose to continue to smoke cigarettes. To me, the behavior is completely irrational, yet I find myself having one from time to time. Those who smoke do so in a rational manner that makes sense in their eyes. Even though smokers inhale toxic smoke into their lungs and poison themselves hourly, they still see the behavior as rational no matter how irrational the rest of us think it is.

All behaviors people commit make sense to them for they are at the centre of their behavior. The key here is determining how to predict and curtail those "rational" behaviors that are harmful to people's lives. There is no such thing as irrational behavior. All behavior is rational when viewed from the goggles of the actor. Their decisions are somewhat unpredictable, yet they are always lawful. But that is the very essence of human behavior: it is lawful, but not necessarily predictable. We are but rough economists traveling through life making decision after decision, some of them made in split seconds. We don't make decisions with calculators: we are human and make human decisions. While these decisions may not be rational to the observer, they sure are to the actor, and that's what counts. Even those who do things that at first blush seem to be costly in our eyes, in reality the behavior is truly a benefit in the actor's mind because only he knows the score. Certain things are done because people feel that it is in their interest no matter what it is. Just as the elements that make up our bodies are in lawful order, so too are the behaviors that emanate from those elements. Call them what you will, to the actor they are all perceived to be rational and done in the pursuit of interest and value.

Whyology

We all perceive the environment a little differently from the next guy or girl. This is because of our genetic filter which translates input from the environment and overlays it with the symbolic value we attribute to things. Things are processed by our senses/brains and ordered uniquely by each individual. Our physical characteristics also play a role in how we react to people and how they react to us. People would react differently to a six-foot tall kid who walked into a fifth grade classroom than a kid of average height. In turn, that tall kid reacts to the other children reacting to him and so on. I sit with certain people I know very well, and I try to predict what they will do next by considering the stimuli in the environment. I try to keep one step ahead of them as I attempt to travel into the future, so to speak, to predict what they will do before they do it. Sounds kind of weird, but it is so true.

Siblings are great test cases for this theory of behavior. Many of us were reared in the same home under the same conditions, sharing similar genes with our siblings. Having the cognitive repertoire of past conditions and observing how those close to us behave in certain situations, or how they react to certain stimuli, instills in us some of the keys to predict behavior. Genes are paramount in this prediction equation. That is the part of the behavioral equation (in the form of a sequence of chemicals) that makes up no less than half of who we are and how we behave. It is our higher level of cognition, given to us by our larger brains via our genetic makeup, which complicates the prediction of human behavior much more so than that of the average lab rat or lower animal form.

However, without the higher level of cognition made possible by our brain size, our behavior would be very predictable and life wouldn't be so interesting. It is the commingling of environmental stimuli with one's genetic "soup" that determines personality and sets in motion future responses based on values that an actor has attributed to things in the environment. If she encounters something new, she will make generalizations/discriminations based on similar stimuli she has previously encountered. This is called stimulus generalization and stimulus discrimination, which are the mirror images of each other. I will discuss this in more detail later.

As discussed, acts of altruism or self-destruction would seem to fly in the face of behavior done for the sake of self interest. However, flipping the perspective, even giving up one's life for something may make

28

economic sense for that person. For example, if a youth commits suicide, we all sit back and think, *how could he have done this?* At its most basic, being dead was more valuable to this person than being alive. At the moment someone arrives at this conclusion, he or she begins to contemplate or attempt to commit suicide.

The best indicator of future suicide is a past attempt. Other predictors of suicide are feelings of helplessness or hopelessness. The aim of treating suicidal individuals is trying to understand the person's values and responses by observing their behaviors and situations. These mental issues can be explored, and if we can show the individual that life is more valuable than death, we will prevent suicide as long as the value of being alive *always* remains more than the value of being dead. That is the essential job of mental health care practitioners. If a patient suffers from a severe mental disorder, then get him or her on proper medications. If there are drug or abuse problems, address these things head-on. But, at the core of treatment, the main goal is to increase the perceived value of being alive rather than dead in the mind of the suicidal actor.

We must elevate life's worth in the mind of the suicidal person who wishes to escape this world because of some mental affliction or other benign reason. No matter how bad it gets, we must instill in the individual that suicide is not an option. The more costly and painful life is perceived to be, the more likely someone is to try to kill him or herself. Suicide is based on self-interest, just as all voluntary behaviors are.

As with any psychopathology or mental disorder, educating the subject on what the possible causes are, and what underlying conditions they may have, is paramount. Education should always be part of any treatment regime when dealing with psychological disorders, as long as patients retain the ability to comprehend and understand the roots of the problem. Treating those with psychological disorders such as anorexia, bulimia, phobias, stress disorders, anxiety, panic attacks and the like all require a good dose of education on the matter. Dialogue with a behavioral expert is key and can alter dangerous behavioral patterns or other behavioral issues. This can only be done after an in-depth interview with the patient.

I urge you to become a scientist yourself and observe the way people move about saying and doing certain things. Always continue to ask yourself *Why?* I challenge the reader not to prove that I'm right, but to prove that my theory is wrong. The more you think about what is said in this book, the more you will have come to your own conclusions about the validity of my theory weighed against your own experiences.

It is the uniqueness and broadness of human behavior that makes it so hard to quantify. We are more complicated than we can appreciate when it comes to things like our subconscious minds. We are using our own brains to study ourselves. We study the behavior of people by watching them and making observations. There is no better place for this than the "laboratory" of everyday life. Psychology is not like physics whereby things can be precisely measured and verified empirically—at least not yet. A good theory in psychology explains and allows us to make predictions using a set of inputs or observations, measured or not. The beauty of this book is that it allows everyday observers to close the predictability gap between what they believe will happen, to what actually happens. This is done by uncovering the variables and universal laws of human behavior.

Think about the possible layers of self-interest behind every action. There is always a reason and lawful explanation for our acts, no matter how irrational someone's behavior seems to be to the observer. People meet one another and avoid others because of perceived costs and benefits. Every single choice, decision, and behavior we enact is all about self-interest.

You should be on your way to becoming a "mad" scientist moving through your environment, testing people and enlightening yourself as to why a specific person said something or did something. You will see life and human behavior much more clearly with the glasses of the psychologist at work in the world's laboratory of everyday life filled with everyday people. Thinking about people's past responses and future needs will give you the necessary equipment for dealing with them—and for furthering your own needs.

We all have our agenda of interests. Live and let live, or the conflicting interests around you will consume you. Even in his pessimism, Hobbes would admit that a stance of civility, tolerance and respect when dealing with our self-interested fellow men keeps these rampant needs in check. In a world where self-interest governs all, our understanding and effort creates a framework of operation where our interests, goals and desires can be attained, while maintaining humility and respect for all.

Behavior is lawful, but not necessarily predictable. However, predictability can become more accurate and likely if we start at a good reference point with the right theory of the laws of human behavior. My theory of biobehaviorism allows us to understand more deeply the roots of human behavior and allows us, more than ever before, to make more accurate predictions of human behavior. When we are equipped with the proper information it tells us **WHY** something happened.

With the right information it *may* also tell us what will happen next. Behavioral observation alone may not always allow us to make accurate predictions because we are human and have internal feelings and bodily functions always at play. These inner states cannot be discounted from the equation even though for the most part they have only small effects on behavior in general. For example, if you know someone well and have a lot of information about a particular situation you'd probably be able to know what kinds of behaviors that person would emit in a particular environmental setting. However, by mere observation there would be nothing to highlight an internal operation that completely derails that person from acting in their stereotypical manner. An actor acting in his stereotypical manner, predictable by the savvy onlooker, might be overshadowed by an internal dilemma in the actor demanding attention, such as that person being extremely thirsty or having to vomit. However, all other things held relatively constant at an internal level, the ability to *explain, predict, and modify* people's behavior is the cornerstone of the reason I wrote this book.

Remember, every single behavior emitted by every single person in every corner of the world is done for a reason and can be explained. Every behavior has purpose. Every behavioral utterance can be broken down and deduced into the elements that made it occur in the first place.

This book brings the vast field of psychology one step closer toward being an "exact science" and brings us closer to the "proof" of human behavior. Find that everyday scientist within yourself as you study the behavior of those in your presence and begin to answer the *why* on your own.

CHAPTER 3 - Science of the Self

This chapter is academic in tone. Although it is a little harder to read than the rest of the book, keep reading. Get through this chapter. It provides a necessary background to where the rest of the book will take you. It will all fall into place.

There have been countless writers on the subject of human behavior and human personality. I was partly inspired to write this book by the many chapters and papers I had read in school on the topics of learning and behavior of all types of organisms. For those of you contemplating going to university or college not knowing if it is worth it, think again. Had it not been for my decision to go to university I would never have collided with the proper environment to unlock my own buried talents, or gained the tools to apply ideas to observation when it came to psychology. The brain is a very powerful and complicated organ, and with the right catalyst many things are possible to accomplish or discover, unless you've been dealt such a disadvantageous genetic hand coupled with a poor environment, leaving you doomed to be behind the eight ball all of your life. However, focusing on the inner workings of the brain and its parts is better left for an anatomy class. Just know that the brain controls all of our actions and converts what we sense in the environment into what we see, hear, feel, smell, and taste. Even if you go to university for four years and nothing ever comes out of it directly, you will be better off in the long run for the trial of it.

Don't get me wrong, school is not for everyone. However, if the opportunity is staring you in the face, don't ever turn it down. You never know what academic treasures you may have buried deep within your mind. It is worth every second. It is even worth the miserable hours when you sit stressed out in the library during final exams, staring at the ceiling and wondering where you'll be in five years. You may wonder how the hell you got to this place, studying on a Friday night while your friends are out having fun. But it is all worth it.

I see the world of human behavior almost in the fourth dimension. Not the fourth dimension as it relates to time. By the fourth dimension, I mean that I am able to envision or observe objects or patterns of behavior from all angles at one time, in a deep mental state. I catch myself in the fourth dimension about once a month and it is a surreal feeling of deep knowledge coupled with a deep understanding of what I am thinking about. It is a sort of energy that overcomes me and I find myself coming out of this weird feeling, trying to recall what was going through my mind.

I was sitting with my friends one day as I slipped into the fourth dimension. I was thinking very deeply about something that was related to behavioral psychology, triggered by something one of my friends said. I was in the fourth dimension for about seven seconds, when I suddenly slipped out and hadn't a clue what I was thinking about. I had to think really deeply about what it was I was thinking and once I remembered, I ran to a pad of paper and jotted down my ideas as my friends looked on, staring at me like I had just been struck by lightning. I don't know what sets it off: it's like entering into a trance of extremely deep thought for a few seconds, swimming in a stream of echoes and understanding. These are the pieces to the final solution of human behavior.

Just as I continued to think about untangling the complex riddle of human behavioral psychology, so too did many great theorists. As such, you need to understand the roots of where my theory of biobehaviorism came from. Biobehaviorism is built upon the foundation of great thinkers in the past. We must be acquainted with them to get a true understanding of human behavior.

Modern psychology cannot escape the influence of Sigmund Freud, who wrote extensively on the topic of human personality and behavior. He believed that much of what was submerged in our unconscious mind played a key role in the actions and troubles of individuals. He has given us some of the names we use for the unseen, labeling the three aspects of the personality as the id, ego and superego, which he asserted governed behavior. These three provinces of the mind are the hallmark of Freud's psychoanalytic theory. These three systems of the mind were believed to be operating in conjunction with one another to push and propel our behavior in one way or another relative to our environmental surroundings and historical inputs.

The id is unconscious and consists of the primitive hardwired drives, instincts and reflexes which comprise who we are because of our biology. The id's main goal is to reduce tension in us by attempting to achieve a level of relative homeostasis or equilibrium. The id acts in a purely hedonistic manner, seeking to attain pleasure and avoid pain or tension. In my view, we are all hedonists at all times no matter where we are, even at the conscious level. However, most of us are hedonistic within boundaries. The id would be like a caveman or a newborn child devoid of cultural norms, boundaries, laws or morality just moving about, satisfying its urges such as hunger, thirst, and excretion in a state of social and mental anarchy. This state of chaos, as Freud called it, has at its core the simple need of instant pleasure, to relieve or cease tension.

The id is the brutal, unpolished portion of who we are. It is the raw and primitive part. It is completely amoral, selfish, egocentric, subjective, and illogical. A baby is the best example of how the id works. A baby is a vessel in pursuit of simple satisfaction, such as food and water. It will do what it deems necessary to reduce tension, such as cry or urinate. It is completely selfish and quickly forms cause and effect associations.

The second system which Freud termed the ego, is born out of the driving forces of the id. The ego creates boundaries which allow the drives of the id to unfold. The ego must steer the inevitable and pressing forces of the id, so that it can reduce tension in an acceptable manner within which the environment will afford us to do so. Its focus is to achieve a workable milieu of behavior based on the real world and the driving forces of the id. The ego must make decisions that will be most suitable to satisfying what the id desires. The ego has a great responsibility in that it must satisfy the forces of the id by environmentally acceptable means, which are not always congruent with the forces of the id.

> The ego is that part of the id which has been modified by the direct influence of the external world ... The ego represents what may be called reason and common sense, in contrast to the id, which contains the passions ... in its relation to the id it is like a man on horseback, who has to hold in check the superior strength of the horse; with this difference, that the rider tries to do so with his own strength, while the ego uses borrowed forces.[1]

As we age, we begin to learn that our primitive urges and drives must be steered and satisfied via socially acceptable channels. We can't walk through a supermarket and eat what we like. We can't attempt to have sex with anyone we like. We must steer these hard-wired drives and desires in a way that is culturally congruent with our context.

The superego is Freud's last system of behavior/personality. The superego stands in opposition of the id. The superego is the mirror image of the id. It is our moral compass. It is our moral conscience, imposed on us by others. Freud believed that through these three systems, we attempt to reduce tension, thereby making us behave in our unique and idiosyncratic ways. He believed that excessive tension or anxiety was dealt with by certain defense mechanisms acting unconsciously. It was the uncovering and unraveling of these buried psychopathological seeds that Freud wanted to unearth and examine, for these were thought to be the seeds which blossomed into our distress.

Freud used methods such as free association to probe into the unconscious mind of the afflicted individual. This entailed the patient sitting in a comfortable environment verbalizing whatever came to his mind, no matter what it was. Any thought was fair game and was encouraged to be put into words. Freud was also very interested in dreams, as they were rich with information housed purely in the unconscious mind. He believed that there was a festering conflict in the unconscious mind that needed to be unearthed and dealt with if one was afflicted mentally.

When building his rubric of psychodynamics, Freud created names for many phenomena that the unconscious mind uses to deal with distress. One such anxiety-reducing process of the unconscious mind is called repression. Freud believed certain thoughts may become repressed or buried into the unconscious, exerting their forces via other routes of behavior. Certain repressed episodes might include events that were traumatic to the actor causing anxiety to be reduced via a subconscious process of burying the experience. Many children who were sexually abused were thought to have repressed thoughts of the abusive episodes in order to cope with them.

With increasing discussion Freud attempted to probe into the unconscious mind of the individual to uncover the submerged thoughts or feelings at the root of the subject's distress. By uncovering these hidden shadows, Freud believed he, the psychoanalyst, could be a guide through the twisted pathways of the mind. He thought that he could aid people through whatever it was they were going through by uncovering and uprooting these embedded mental pathologies housed in the unconscious mind. Even though Freud would label himself as an empiricist, his focus on the metaphysical has attracted much criticism. Yet the attention garnered by his work remains cult-like.

Freud asserted that psychology would never become an exact science; however, advances in genetics and computer technology are daily bringing the proof of human behavior and psychology closer to the rigor of empirical science. Psychology may never become an *exact* science in the way that physics is, but our ability to explain and predict human behavior will become increasingly likely, reliable, and valid as more is known about our genetic codes, and as advancements in technology allow us to process ever-growing reams of information. As commentators such as Hall and others have suggested, "The fact of the matter is that all theories of behavior are pretty poor theories and all of them leave much to be desired in the way of scientific proof. Psychology has a long way to go before it can be called an exact science."[2]

Freud didn't give enough credit to our genetic codes as he overemphasized the buried treasures located in the unconscious mind. What Freud didn't attribute much of our behavior to, was our locked-in genetic predispositions that magnetize us to certain parts of our environment in an idiosyncratic manner. Our genetic codes determine the vessel that we will travel through life with. This vessel is as individual as our faces and "decides" much of our behavior. Our genetic codes create the vehicle in which we navigate our world.

We all start on the starting line with our soup of genes, much like a racecar starts on the track before a race begins. Our behavior will be determined mainly by our genetic codes, analogous to a specific car sitting on a racetrack revving up. Some of us will start the race in a Mercedes. Some of us will start the race in a Ferrari, and some will start the race in a Ford Pinto. The unfortunate ones will start the race in a go-kart. Our idiosyncratic vehicles make up a huge part of who and what we are, and who we will ultimately become. They influence the process by which we react to environmental stimuli, playing a huge role in what we are attracted to, be it music or the opposite sex.

No two people see exactly the same thing at once, so the same stimulus affects everyone in slightly different ways. Remember that past encounters matter too. Freud would argue that the variability and uniqueness of human behavior are derived from the ways in which a person attempts to reduce tension. I would say that our diversity, uniqueness, and variability is fixed at birth—or more correctly, these are fixed once our genetic code is determined in the womb, with half of our genes coming from our father and the other half from our mother. Learning and consequent behavior has to do with finding out what we perceive to be valuable to us in the environment, attributing value to those things as we look through the prism of our genetic code and historical context.

Freud believed tension reduction guided our behavior. Tension reduction is just half of the equation. Tension reduction is analogous to negative reinforcement, which is the removal of a negative stimulus that causes people to behave similarly in the future toward the factor that eliminated that negative stimulus. For example, if you had sunburn and put on aloe which removed the pain, you would be more likely to commit that behavior in the future because it reduced or eliminated a negative stimulus. This same future behavior is a negatively reinforcing act for reduce tension.

However, people behave in certain ways when there is no tension at all, as in the realm of positive reinforcement. Committing a behavior such as mowing the lawn for your dad for money is most likely positive reinforcing because it will increase the likelihood of the behavior happening again. In this case, the money is a positive reinforcer for mowing the lawn.

Freud had some great ideas, and I can't really knock him because, at the time of his writing, genetics was in its infancy. However, he thought ahead of the curve for his time, elevating him to celebrity status among his peers and society in general. Freud's novel theory is quite interesting as it relates to the personality and behavior of humans. Freud's id, ego, and superego, as he termed the different provinces of the brain that composed the personality and drove behavior is an overly simplistic division of the complex interaction among neurological and genetic elements.

Freud focused too closely on theoretical energy distributions of the "systems of the mind." He has been criticized by many for failing to enter the realm of true experimental psychology by employing controlled experiments. This is where Freud and I join paths. Like Freud, I consider myself to be an empiricist, yet I do not point to controlled experimental data as a basis for my theory of human behavior. And neither could Freud. We base our theories on the countless observations of the human condition and the human subject behaving in the real world. It is from these intense observations that our theories are born. My theory of biobehaviorism is not based on controlled experimental research per se. It is based on a multitude of behavioral observations in the field of human behavior in the "laboratory" of our everyday world.

I crave the study of behavior in its purest, most unadulterated form—that is, by observing people who don't know they are being studied in the real world. Only then can true observation and deductions of human behavior be studied on its lawful path. By "lawful path," I mean the inevitable actions of mankind based on a set of stimuli they lawfully react to. By knowing this, we can deduce why a certain behavior was committed, which will assist us in predicting future behavior. This is a very powerful tool in behavioral modification.

Arguably, some behavior cannot be experimentally verified because invoking controls in the study of human behavior, as in the basis of empirical study, would upset the natural flow of human behavior and interaction. Thus, I make continuous observations in the "field" of human behavior by observing the behavior of people as they go about their daily lives, thereby validating my theory for myself and for you. Like Freud and his psychoanalytic sessions, I believe modifying behavior and treating afflicted individuals can best be achieved through individual contact.

A differing school of psychology emerged with B.F. Skinner at the forefront. Behavioral psychology was revolutionized by the work of Skinner and his infamous rats.[3] Skinner was vehemently against the explanation of behavior in terms of cognitive processes; instead, he focused on motivation as manifested in physical response. In his view, it was a fruitless endeavor to attempt to match behavior to unseen metaphysical mental cognitive processes.

Skinner's model of behavior has at its core a paradigm of positive and negative reinforcement mechanisms that he thought governed behavior and could be used to condition organisms. It was reinforcement, he asserted, that would make the behaviors leading to that reinforcement more likely to occur in the future. The other side of the equation is made up of punishment and response cost, things that would make behavior less likely to occur in the future. If subjects were punished, they'd be less likely to commit the same behavior that led to their punishment (like when a child is spanked for doing something wrong). Response cost occurs when a behavior or set of behaviors causes a subject to lose something of value, thereby making the behaviors leading up to the loss less likely to occur in the future. An example would be a teenager losing the keys to his parents' car because of bad behavior.

In its simplest form, reinforcers are valuable because they either bring us something of value by our actions (positive reinforcement—such as money) or they take something we don't like away (negative reinforcement—such as aloe on a sunburn). When we are reinforced by getting value—money or relief—we are more likely to commit these behaviors in the future because we are all value seekers. The flip side is a loss of value, either by committing an action that brings punishment or one that loses value. When we are punished or lose value (being spanked or losing the keys to the parents' car), we are less likely to commit behaviors that cost us that value. Due to these effects behavior is conditioned by value lost or achieved. Skinner would contend that something is a reinforcer only if the reinforcer makes that behavior which led up to getting it more likely to occur in the future, i.e., it reinforces the behavior. I would argue that anything deemed valuable by an actor is reinforcing and an actor would always strive to attain that value because behavior is reinforced by value. These processes have extremely powerful implications for how we behave and how we can change for the better.

Skinner meticulously measured the effects of positive and negative reinforcement using a contraption called the "Skinner Box," wherein he would measure the responses of select organisms, such as rats, in a controlled experimental study in order to quantify their behavior. Unlike Freud, Skinner was an experimental psychologist. Skinner believed in lawful structures: that the *consequences* of past behavior governed a subject's behavior in the future. As well, by dealing with motivations of hunger and thirst, Skinner's experiments linked biology to psychology. However, Skinner's method views biological factors as consistent and common across subjects, whereas I would argue genetics predispose us to giving certain things value in the environment and make biological factors of behavior *inconsistent* among subjects. An example would be someone who is lactose intolerant (like myself) solely because of genetic factors and behaves in a certain way solely because of that fact, all else being equal. Nonetheless,

Skinner gave enough credit to the fact that genetics predispose us to giving certain things value in the environment.

I believe, as Skinner did, in the lawfulness of behavior. Skinner also could not discount the biological underpinnings of behavior entrenched in us via our specific DNA message. Hall and others have suggested that "In the first place, [Skinner] argued that an organism's sensitivity to reinforcement itself has a genetic basis."[4] Further,

> He also recognized that some behaviors may have a completely genetic basis, so that experience will have no effect on them. Skinner saw a parallel between the hereditary and environmental bases of behavior.[5]

We are predisposed to value certain things more than others purely because of genetics. Skinner and his behavioral paradigm of psychology has been one of the most studied areas of psychology in modern time. Skinner's theories have been applied to a multitude of bad habits, social ills, and other behavioral problems.

Of all the psychologists, my psychological ideology falls most in line with those statements of B.F. Skinner and only slightly with Freud's. I am in agreement with Freud in that we can understand and extrapolate the elements of behavior by studying the individual. I am a behaviorist at my core though. However, certain elements acting in the unconscious realm cannot be assigned zero weight, as much as Skinner would love to assign them zero credit in the behavioral world. I am a biobehaviorist though, because I believe that as much as emphasis is given to genetic predisposition to govern behavior, the same emphasis must be given to environmental propellers of action, such as positive reinforcers. Moreover, as Hall and his colleagues emphasize, "Skinner, like Freud, deserves recognition for his constant emphasis on the orderliness of behavior."[6] These theorists just differ on how that order is brought about. They argued, as I do, that behavior is orderly and follows lawful paths. That is the starting point for understanding, observing, controlling, and predicting behavior. I owe much of my psychological inspiration to Skinner in that his writings and experimental control of behavior created a massive amount of raw psychological ore for future explorers to reconcile.

Like many theorists of human behavior, Skinner, like Freud, was the target of much criticism. One such critic of Skinner was Noam

Chomsky, the famous linguist. He was quick to discount Skinner's theory and his behaviorist views because of an obscure behavioral phenomenon evidenced in lower animals called instinctual drift. This term was coined by Breland and Breland after they conducted a well-known experiment with raccoons in 1961.[7] In the experiment food was used to positively reinforce (reward) raccoons for picking up a coin and dropping it into a metal container. After a while they noticed that the raccoons were deviating or drifting from those behaviors that led to produce the reinforcer (food) by picking up a coin and dropping it in the box. The Brelands noticed that as training went on the raccoons (and other animal species) would instinctively drift away from the behaviors they were reinforced to perform. The Brelands observed the raccoons rubbing the coins together and holding them firmly, which were instinctive behaviors of food washing in raccoons.

This superimposed intrusion of hard-wired instinctual behavioral tendencies in the right conditions in no way dilutes the efficacy of Skinner's behaviorist model as Chomsky believed it did. Skinner set out and showed what he intended to achieve in numerous experiments. He displayed over and over that reinforcement could modify, manipulate, and control behavioral patterns in many different animal species to a large degree. Skinner modified and controlled the behavior of animals by observing and reinforcing them for eliciting the behaviors he desired. He could condition animals to behave in certain ways using reinforcers such as food. This was called operant or Skinnerian conditioning. Just because the organisms displayed hard-wired species specific food related behaviors from time to time during conditioning does not throw the behaviorism paradigm out the window.

Skinner did not contend that these animals he experimented with were on a remote control. Skinner himself asserted that certain behaviors were governed mainly by genetics, such as species specific rituals or behaviors. There will always be instinctual leakage with any organism in a Skinnerian conditioning milieu. Thus Skinner's model is correct, but some may argue it is incomplete. Domjan, and others, suggest that behavior patterns can exceed what we see in the lab: "The Brelands emphasized that such instinctive response tendencies have to be taken into account in the analysis of behavior."[8] Behaviorism is alive and well, however, it is lacking in its emphasis on predispositions emanating from our biology, which is at the core of our behavior as humans. Hence, my theory accounts for this shortfall in Skinner's model and is aptly named biobehaviorism because our genetic predispositions and idiosyncrasies are always part of the behavioral proof.

Perfectly accurate predictions of human behavior are virtually impossible due to environmental externalities and the limitless combinations of our genetic cloaks. It is not that behavior is unpredictable per se; it is just that externalities are inherently unpredictable, thus making behavior unpredictable because we react to these externalities in unique ways. It is easy to calculate how much force would be needed to direct a certain object to a certain place, as a physicist could easily predict. But how could you predict, with certainty, what a person would do if he encountered the variable x (whatever we want that to be) in a certain situation. However, whatever reactions a person has to a particular stimulus are *always* lawful. A psychology professor at Brown University has commented:

> The laws of learning and behavior are always in effect, like Newton's laws of gravity and Ohm's law of electrical circuitry. Our knowledge of them and their implications may be uncertain or incomplete, and await further discoveries, but that is so in all sciences.[9]

All behavior is lawful, but not necessarily predictable. It is the bridging of this gap between the lawfulness of behavior and its predictability which is the challenge of modern psychology today. As that gap closes, psychology will move ever closer to the realm of becoming an exact science. Only when we get closer to pinning down all of the right variables of human behavior may we better be able to predict it. The more we know about our subject, including genetics and historical context, the closer we can come to predicting what a person will do next in a given situation, or how they will respond to a particular stimulus when they encounter it. For example, what would your friend do if he walked into a room and saw a large spider crawling on the wall? He might freak out, or he might dismiss it as nothing, or he might kill it, or he might chase you with it. It will be that person's historic context and genetic milieu that will determine how they will react. If your friend has an innate or predisposed fear of spiders, and has never liked them or coped with them environmentally, then he will probably not react favorably to the sight of a large spider creeping towards him.

Everyone has hard-wired fears that accompany each of us into the world. We all are predisposed to fear certain things. There are thousands of different phobias, from the common to the obscure, that afflict people. Due to the fact that many of these fears are hard-wired, psychologists must tap into the environmental end of the behavioral matrix to help people overcome those fears by a milieu of techniques. Some fears may be conditioned as well, which makes them easier to overcome.

Many people have anxieties to certain things in the environment, or people may be anxious generally. We can almost always thank our genetic codes for our irrational fears and anxieties that afflict us on a daily basis. Some people suffer from anxiety disorders purely because of genetics, they are anxious because they inherited "anxious genes." For these people anxiety is a part of the mosaic of who they are. On the environmental side of the equation, we may combat these hard-wired tendencies using things such as exercise, meditation, education, therapy, and so on.

When attempting to conquer or manage a certain addiction or phobia, the problem is that since genetics is always at a constant we cannot modify someone's idiosyncratic predisposition to that addiction or phobia in the course of treatment. However, we must strive to educate and alter the behavioral models and schedules of reinforcement of an afflicted person to give them the tools to cope with or conquer the problem.

I was sitting at a friend's place when someone I knew well returned from the casino. This casino dweller looked wired as if he was high on drugs. Well he was: he was high from his own body's response to the thrill of gambling. It was his rush. He loved it. I know of no other person who gets this reaction from games of chance and exposure to variable schedules of reinforcement. Many true alcoholics fall into addiction partly because of genetic predisposition. That is why treating some of them can be very difficult. Some would even go as far to say that they have a disease. I think not. That would be like saying a rapist or a pedophile had a disease, when they do not, although they may be able to point, with merit, to strong genetic precursors as the impetus and root cause of their unacceptable behavior. That is why some of these people are virtually impossible to treat and rehabilitate. There is only so much that a psychologist can do in altering and helping those in need. Only with knowledge of the true building blocks and ingredients of behavior can we attempt to alter the behavioral patterns that allow someone's addictions or phobias to control him or her.

My job is to put you in control. An actor is not in control if their vice or psychopathology is in control of them. Ask yourself: do you have control of the addiction or vice you have, whatever it may be? Can you resist it in the face of temptation? Does it disrupt your regular day-to-day life, including your work and family life, to an intolerable level? If so, you are out of control and something has control over you.

Never lose control. When you have lost control you are at the mercy of your environment and whatever it has planned for you. For you are a slave to that harmful value you foolishly choose to chase. We must understand where we stand relative to our continuous and persistent vice chasing. Stop it right there. Understand why you do what you do. Get control of it and resist it; be that champion and make yourself proud. I always try to remain in control in all that I do. I must be. Losing control puts you at the mercy of chasing dangerous value down many unpredictable paths that could get you into deep trouble.

The first step in any treatment regime should be education after an in-depth interview and diagnosis. Following this, there should be a slow calculated process toward a goal. Sometimes cold turkey works, but it's the hardest method on the organism and requires the greatest discipline. Something as plaguing as obesity, which afflicts millions in Canada and the USA, could be easily reversed with education and simple behavioral manipulation. We in North America must get control of ourselves as we are seen by the world as gluttonous over-consumers. Behavior is a complicated matter with many variables that must be taken into account to modify its negative aspects.

The predictability of human behavior is further complicated by the existence of the unconscious system of the mind. Most of what we have experienced is "locked" away in our unconscious mind. The unconscious houses countless fragments of different memories and thoughts, faces, fears, and desires. Just what our brains decide to house there is very hard to determine, but we can be sure that there is a process by which our brains house this material. Further, only under the right conditions will certain information in the unconscious mind cross the permeable "membrane" and enter the conscious mind. Try a memory as an example. Think back many years to a relatively benign experience that happened to you at the age of eight, roundabout the third grade. Think back to what you were doing, what you remember about your house, about the media, about school, about your friends, your parents, and so on. Your memory is probably pretty selective because it is hard to think deeply and uncover those really trivial memories, even though many trivial memories and faces of a lot of people you have seen in your lifetime are buried in your subconscious mind.

Not long ago, I had a dream about a woman. I was having dinner with my brothers the next day, and I asked them if they thought if it was possible for someone to see the face of another so clearly and distinctively in their dream without seeing that person in real life. The consensus was that I had to have seen that woman before *somewhere*, even if for only a split second. I was still unsure because of the unique ability of our brains to fill in gaps of history with mental foliage. But I wanted to push the thought forward and see if a "memory" could be induced. I said, "Let's picture in our minds a Caucasian male with a brown moustache, blue eyes, long hair, and a long nose. Is it possible that my mind just created this woman as I just created this imaginary man in my head?" Maybe. On the other hand, I may have seen the woman before and the immense power of my sensitive brain encoded her face so well into my subconscious mind that for whatever reason she became a piece of my mental repository. Or was I wrong? Was it possible that the face was a culmination of different people's faces that were molded together in my head to produce this mystery woman, giving me a memory assembled from unrelated components? This is possible, too. This is the problem with the subconscious mind: its very nature and complexity leaves questions to be answered.

Even in its natural form, the unconscious mind is very unpredictable in what it stores and what it allows to seep into the conscious realm. That ties into the reason that the prediction of human behavior in a precise manner poses great difficulty, keeping psychology out of the "club" of the empirical sciences. So, when you are asleep and having a nasty nightmare about spiders crawling on your pillow, and you suddenly awake, the memory and sensation left by traces of the dream will no doubt make you behave in a certain way, even if only for a short time. The unconscious mind, by its own power and reasons propels your behavior in the instant of waking and sets off a chain of conscious reaction. That cannot be predicted based on genes and historical context, not now at any rate. This undoubtedly throws a curveball into nailing down the proof of human behavior with genetics and historical context as the key elements of that proof.

Freud's attention to the unconscious mind is a foundational concept of both the research and the practice of psychology today. The classic analogy of the mind being like an iceberg with most of the mind submerged in the unconscious (underwater), and only the conscious tip protruding, continues to hold some validity. Our unconscious mind never rests, and when we fall asleep or are knocked unconscious, the conscious mind, like the tip of the iceberg, becomes submerged into the unconscious realm. It is on standby waiting to be used again. Our conscious and unconscious mind, operating in tandem, act as our day-to-day operating system, guiding us along the path in the struggle to pursue our interests.

Our conscious mind is the compass of life, inextricably linked to our five senses, as it processes the world around us, pushing and pulling us towards items of perceived value. The unconscious part of the mind houses past experiences gleaned from our senses. We file these experiences away in our mental libraries in the unconscious realm to lie dormant until they are needed for application in the conscious mind. Our conscious mind is the highest state of consciousness and involves a heightened state of awareness of what we see in our environment.

We are able to rationalize from an early age by watching and doing what will bring us pleasure and what will bring us harm. We learn as our predispositions, predetermined by genetic variance, collide with the environment awaiting us from the moment we exit the womb. Certain early life experiences affect certain things we do as we age, such as deep-rooted phobias. However, these form only a small piece of our behavioral mosaic in the way they influence our future behavior. Watch how your son or daughter walks or chews his or her food, or how your parents eat their food. You will have strong commonalities with close family members based purely on genetic foundations.

Freud's contributions to the subject of psychology will never be forgotten for he was a pioneer in laying down some foundational concepts of personality, human behavior and the unconscious mind. His focus on elements in the unconscious realm has several implications in the field of psychology to this day. However, it is my strong belief that the study of the unconscious mind is only a small slice into the realm of human behavior. Freud's overemphasis on the unconscious mind has only served to dilute the efficacy of his theory and made him more susceptible to attack. However, at a time when genetics was in its infancy, he didn't have full access to the workings of the biological side of the equation. He inspired thought and dialogue (just as I attempt to do here) and added many great ideas to the world of psychology. For this, I applaud him. However, it was Skinner who was closest to the mark when it came to understanding and explaining all human behavior.

Freud and Skinner were instrumental in the field of psychology. Their theories have been applied to real life situations in an attempt to assist those suffering certain psychopathologies, including addiction, obesity, hoarding, anorexia, and obsessive compulsive disorders. The value of personal connection and close understanding is a valuable part of observation. As we interact with others in the everyday laboratory, the psychoanalytic and behaviorist tools of observation, discussion and questioning will be of great value in gathering practical knowledge. These tools will also be of value in cracking the proof of human behavior once and for all. Professor Lipsitt sums up this idea neatly: "Just as natural laws form the basis of the sciences of physics and chemistry, laws describing and explaining the regularities of human behavior also exist."[10]

CHAPTER 4 - Who Am I and Where Am I Going?

A few years ago, my uncle passed away, and my large family was at the burial site. Some of my family members were crying out loud, and others were mourning quite stoically. Some of the people around me were emotionless statues just standing there, not saying a word. I found it quite disturbing (and interesting) that they were not breaking down. However, the more I thought about it, the more it made sense to me. Our grieving processes are as idiosyncratic as our faces. We all grieve in different ways. We do so mainly because of our genetic inheritances, temperament and partly because of our previous experiences.

We are malleable beings to a certain degree. Our personalities are like water, having the same elemental composition yet moving and acting in their own unique fluidity. The possibilities of who we may become chases infinity because of our endless pursuit for what we perceive as valuable in the multitude of contexts we find ourselves, and the almost endless possibilities of our genetic combinations. When we inherit our genetic soup from our parents, we get some enduring traits that express who we are, just like the genes that express the color of our eyes. In the world of psychology, we call someone's general behavioral theme or state their temperament. It is the "face" of who we are, the intangible, unimaginable face that lurks within us.

Some people's temperaments are serious; some are jovial; some are edgy; some are happy. What's yours? How would you describe yours if you were asked? How would your friends or family describe your temperament?

Our temperaments are mostly governed by our genetic codes, which are unique to each human being. Just as no two humans share the exact same genetic code (not even identical twins), no two people share the same temperament. There are, however, generalizations we make whereby we group different people as having a certain type of temperament because of commonalities they share. So, if we were to compare two people and they were generally happy people, extroverted and similar in demeanor, we would say that they had temperament X as opposed to Y, mainly because of the genetic hand they were dealt and, more subtly, because of their interactions with their environment.

Closely tied to temperament are our predispositions. Predispositions are predetermined inclinations or preferences for certain things in our environment. Alternatively, we may be more susceptible to some things in the world than others because of our genes. For example, simply based on genetics alone, someone may be predisposed to really liking alcohol and becoming addicted to it. This is just another example of our genetics determining to a large part how we behave and who we will become.

Predispositions stem purely from genetics. For the most part, no two humans share the same temperament or predispositions in how they behave in the game of life. As I described earlier, every human being starts his or her journey in an idiosyncratic vessel, much like a particular race car starts a race. Each car is as unique and individual as the next. Each car (or vessel) has its specific engines, tires, suspension, aerodynamics, and paint job. Before the race, the cars have no experience on the track. When the light goes green, it is like the day we exit our mother's womb. Two virtually identical cars, just like identical twins, will start the race in almost identical vehicles and positions, but after hundreds of laps each car (even identical ones) will have its own unique wear and tear.

Our temperament is the way we are, on average, in our normal day-to-day life. Even though our temperaments are, on average, the way they are because of genes, they can be swayed by our interactions with the environment. That sway has limits, however, due to the strong enduring result of the expression of our temperaments via our genetics, which will determine the outer areas of the temperamental core.

My temperament is somewhat serious, even though I joke around at times. That doesn't prevent people from asking me why I'm so serious all of the time. I was predisposed to "be" a certain way in my relatively tensionless mental state. What is your temperament in *your* average resting state? How much sway has your temperament endured because of your environmental experiences?

Human personality and behavior are dynamic and fluid concepts that are continuously changing because of our continual interaction with the evolving external world and our biology (genetics). What remain constant are our enduring genetic traits, such as those that crystallize our temperaments, and more importantly, those that form the building blocks of our personalities and predispositions. While certain genes may be turned on at different points in our lives, the core genetic soup remains highly determinative of our actions.

There are, however, certain life experiences that can push us to the outer edges of our temperamental cores. Certain traumatic events, such as returning from the battlefield or experiencing assault may cause what is known as post-traumatic stress disorder. Those traumatic experiences cause a person's temperament to sway away from his or her core or resting or average temperament. A very traumatizing event causes such a strong shock to the senses that the affected person deviates from his or her resting temperamental state to the outer edges of their normal range. The context for reinforcement becomes damaged because the actor who has experienced this trauma is confused about how to act when drawing on past experiences comprised of non-traumatic experiences mixed with the more recent events of a traumatic experience. Traumatic events also become firmly entrenched in the unconscious mind and are prone to leak into our dreams. Many people who have suffered from a very traumatic experience often have recurring nightmares as the unconscious attempts to reconcile the experience due to its mental saliency relative to pre-existing mental patterns.

Right off the bat, we can attribute a lot of the traits in our personalities to those of our parents. Again, you get half of your genes from your mother and the other half from your father. Genes are of utmost importance. The balance will be determined by our environmental experiences. So, a good part of the character of our personalities is at a constant, set by our genes. It is set like the character of your face. It was determined by a random selection of genes that your parents put together when the sperm met the egg in your mother's womb. Your personality traits are a blend of those constant genetic manifestations that you are not in control of, coupled with what you have experienced to date, via your senses.

The genetic code that forms part of the mosaic of our personalities is like a tattoo on our brains, inked in by the genes we have inherited from our parents. These genes are the hand you have been dealt for the rest of your life. If you are lucky enough to inherit advantageous genes you've won the genetic lottery. If you come from a gene pool that lacks intelligence or doesn't carry genes that are advantageous in your environment, there is absolutely nothing you can change about that. The rest of the equation is up to you. That is determined solely by the environment you have been exposed to, which encompasses the people you have met, the places you have seen, the things (good and bad) that have happened to you, and so on.

The impact of our genes is reflected in our encounters with the external world. Our brains process the input that comes from the environment and fit it within our genetic outline, slowly shaping who we will become on the environmental side of the coin. Our soup of genes will inevitably affect how we interact with the environment and how our environment reacts to us. Life, individuality, personality, and behavior are all nurture and nature. Together, the constant interplay of our genes and environment create the unique picture of who we are.

Personality is something that is forged over many years of life. Personality is not a static concept; it is dynamic, slowly evolving outside of our control. Our personalities change as we experience more and more in life through our 'geneavior,' that part of our behavior governed solely by genetics. Our personalities are simply shaped by our constant geneavior mixed with our experiences with the environment via the sources of input from our five senses. That is what simply makes you who you are. We get to that point, like this very second, by thinking about who we come from and where we've been and what we've experienced through our senses. But what is an experience without a sense? It doesn't exist. There can be no experiences without senses. If you couldn't feel, smell, see, taste, or hear, you wouldn't experience anything. Only with those experiences are we motivated and driven on a life-long journey of the never-ending aim of self-interest. If we could not experience the world through our senses, or even one of them—our behavior would solely be governed by our geneavior.

I'd like you to close your eyes for a second and imagine that your whole body could not feel anything, see anything, hear anything, taste, or smell anything whatsoever. You would be nothing more than an organic shell, driven only by the instincts hard-wired into you.

I propose that if two humans with identical genetic codes were free falling in black space at the moment of birth, with no light, sound, taste, smell, or touch, the twins' behavior would be solely governed by genes (geneavior) and their movements would be identical. They would have to be exact copies of each other, devoid of minor genetic mutations, subject to the exact same developmental noise. Or would they behave exactly the same? Would they make the exact same movements? I want you to think about that. We will revisit this proposition later on. My uncle would say that they wouldn't act the same because their souls are different.

If the human race became infertile this second, and we waited nine months for all the newly pregnant mothers to have their children, and no more people were brought into this world, it might be theoretically calculable to predict the future behavior of every being on this earth until the last person died (holding externalities at a constant). This may sound farfetched, but I believe it should be theoretically possible to roughly predict the behavior of every single human being as they interact with each other and their environments. I mean this in the abstract sense: there is yet no super computer that could calculate this. On a practical level, only a rough prediction of behavior is possible at this time. If the human race suddenly became infertile by a virus that sterilized all of humanity, the human behavior that would unravel from that point on would theoretically be finite and traceable.

As we now stand, as long as we start with the presumption that humans will always be fertile, the count of potential human behaviors is vast, approaching infinity, constantly exposed to externalities in the game of life.

Working from the idea that the formula for future behavior is developed by plugging in the variables of past experience and genetics poses a problem in predicting how one would behave when one encounters a situation that one has never before been exposed to. This is what I mean when I speak of externalities. They are those events or variables in life over which we have no control and do not see coming, such as cancer or tsunamis. There is no readily available legend that tells us, "When Person X has genes a, c, t, y, x and z, they will do f when they encounter g." It is like asking yourself what people you know really well might do if you decided to dye your hair blue. What would the reaction of your mother be? You have a rough idea, because you know a little about how she has reacted to certain situations before, and you kind of know how her personality has been forged and what she values. Her reaction would be somewhat predictable.

Soon, we will become so knowledgeable about our genetic codes that we will be able to predict with greater certainty how someone will react to a particular environmental stimulus, even though he or she has never before encountered it. We will, of course, need some context about where that person has been and what he or she has experienced in his or her life, because behavior is all about the interplay between genes and experiences. The goal is to close the gap between what we predict someone's behavior to be, and what it actually is upon encountering certain stimuli. Our reactions to stimuli will always be lawful, but not entirely predictable.

Unpredictable externalities, such as disaster and disease are examples of the missing variables that make the exact prediction of human behavior to a precise point difficult because these are variables that emerge pretty much from nowhere, and their prediction is virtually impossible. However, that doesn't mean that one's behavior in reaction to an unpredictable event is not lawful. All behavior is lawful, whether the precipitating event was expected or not. That is the key here. Thus, we can still predict reactions to particular stimuli with some accuracy, but we can't foretell future events. There is an important distinction here. You cannot predict if a tornado will demolish your house. However, your reaction to the event will be lawful and somewhat predictable—for example, sending you running to the ditch in your yard or to the basement. Externalities such as a tornado, tsunami or cancer make life unravel in variable ways, much like the variation in our genetic codes.

When I speak of predicting human behavior, I mean it in a mechanical sense, with little weight given to unpredictable externalities. If the world were in a vacuum-like state, we'd be able to map everything out; but then we wouldn't be human, and the world wouldn't exist as we know it.

With the vast number of genetic vessels out there, things can go wrong in how we interact with our environments and how we behave. I don't like when psychologists say that someone has certain features that can be seen or that are absent, as if they either have something or they don't, if they exhibit certain qualities or traits, such as "lacking empathy" or "reactive". When I use the word "traits," I mean it in a looser, more casual sense than clinicians. I don't like terms like "psychopath" that label individuals by symptoms instead of actions. Psychology must and should be understood on gradients or continuums. We categorize people in psychology out of necessity, because existing treatment models depend on clear explanations, labels, diagnoses, and targets. Nonetheless, shifting continuums or gradients are the only way to truly understand people on a psychological level.

If we took a group of sociopaths or psychopaths and sat among them, they would be very different from one another. They each represent their own definitive and finite genetic soups coupled with their previous environmental clashes. However, we look at the group as a whole and lump them together without accounting for individuality: they are just psychopaths. Such erroneous propositions thwart proper intervention to whatever behavioral disorder one is attempting to understand and treat. These dichotomous exercises may be just as harmful to the subject's treatment regimen as they are helpful. Many ready-to-label psychologists superimpose traits on their patients, leading to all the negative consequences of labeling, such as self-fulfilling prophecies and erosion of the patient's self-identity. This may result in inappropriate treatment regimens.

People must be understood and treated, if necessary, on a case-by-case basis, uncovering and understanding their history, genes, reinforcement patterns, values and traits on psychological continuums. Continuums themselves have labels at each end of their spectrums. However, it still gets us out of the pattern of calling someone "X" or "Y" based on what the observer believes he has ferreted out of the person he is labeling. With continuums, we say that someone *tends* to be like this or that as a matter of degree rather than a matter of absolute type or kind. No one person is the same, and no one personality disorder or psychological problem is the same for every person.

Using the classic description of psychopathy, we make a diagnosis by asking if a particular person displays (or lacks) a particular behavioral trait such as a "lack of empathy for others." If we take two similar people and label both as "psychopaths," we might be overlooking the degree of empathy in each person: one may lack it completely while the other may have limited feeling. Thus, it would be correct to think of them as having different degrees of empathy for their fellow man, however slight that may be, as opposed to saying that they both "lack empathy." Their capacities for empathy may be very different and elicited in different circumstances. Classifying people like this works well in practice, and it allows those in the field of psychology to make sense of loosely grouped people who, on the surface, share certain similar touches of certain traits: a pinch of this trait, and some of that trait.

If we say that two people have Disorder X, they lose their individuality. They lose those idiosyncrasies that make them who they are and that shape the manifestation of their personalities. If one had absolutely no empathy and the other person had very little, we would just toss a label on both of them as "not empathetic" and that little empathy the one person had would be left out of the equation of what makes them unique. Remember, personality is fluid. There are no sharp demarcating lines. It's all gradients, continuums, degrees, wild charts, and equations.

To understand the vast range of personalities, I encourage you to people watch. If we want to understand and explain human behavior, we must study it in its unaltered form. Just watch how life unfolds right before your eyes. Just let life be life and watch the people around you. Try to step one second ahead of time by watching, learning and predicting. The more you watch someone, the more you can predict his or her behavior, especially if you are acquainted with someone's gene pool. If you know some history of their behavior, what is important to them (what they value), and begin to plot out some commonalities, you can stay a second ahead of them and determine their angles so you don't get exploited.

Human exploitation is just a matter of one individual being subject to another's self interest. If those around you exploit you and take advantage of you, they don't value much of what you think or how you feel. Your wants and desires don't even enter the equation. It is all about *me, me, me*. But you can still satisfy your self-interest and uphold the value of others by understanding the balance between you. People often take advantage of their friends in ways that are not good. They go too far without giving something in exchange. This will inevitably catch up to the one who is in "debt" with their friends. Think about that the next time you tell a friend something. What you tell them is immediately processed by their self-interest machine: *How does that affect me?*

When I tell a funny story, people might become interested and laugh. However, when I tell someone what I did at work or what I accomplished, they don't really care. Nobody wants to hear that I closed a deal today and made a nice chunk of change. Nobody cares unless they are getting something from it or unless it is in their interest for me to do well. I think the only people who truly care if you do something good are your parents, siblings and other close family members. Otherwise, you are just disrupting people's sense of themselves and their own status.

As I sit with a group of friends, I really watch the conversation and how people react to each other. The reason people are so interested in what I have to say when I'm telling a funny story is because it is in their interest to listen. This is because I make them laugh or make the stories suspenseful.

Watch people as they move, piece by piece, 1.6 second frame by 1.6 second frame, as part of a billion piece set. Tick tick tick…as the seconds go by, self-interest is always at play. Self-interest, coupled with our core inherited personality markers, governs what our personality will become. Our genes remain constant throughout the process, giving us the biological instincts and drives that push us along in self-interested ways that we all behave by. We are continually seeking what we perceive as valuable based on past experience.

On this subject, I was having a conversation with my cousin about idiosyncratic behavior. He was too ready to discount genes in the determination of human behavior whereas I was stressing their paramount importance above all else in how we behave. I lived in the same neighborhood with my cousin for 20 years. Our family lives were very similar and we were exposed to many of the same things. I used an example that he could grasp and that I could prove my point with: sunflower seeds. Ever since I was a young boy, I had a real liking for sunflower seeds. I remember riding my bicycle to the store and getting a bag of sunflower seeds almost every day. I am eating some as I write this paragraph.

I posed a question to my cousin. "What is it about me that makes me love sunflower seeds so much?" He offered a few possible answers, which I shot down. I explained to him that growing up, I was not exposed to sunflower seeds any more than he or my four brothers, yet I came to love the seeds so much that I couldn't stand to be apart from them. I explained to him that since our environments were pretty much at a constant for exposure to sunflower seeds, the only other variable that could produce such a strong effect was that I had a built-in liking for sunflower seeds that was beyond the average. I explained that there is something in my genetic makeup that endowed me with the faculties to really value sunflower seeds. Eating them brought a lot of value to me. This was inextricably linked to my genetic code. My cousin looked at me with a sense of defeat. "Yeah, I guess that makes a lot of sense."

A friend once asked me, "How is it that we grew up almost literally in the same family environments, yet we are going in such different directions in life?" The only logical and correct answer to his question, unbeknownst to him, was the independent variable of the genetic soups we absorbed from our parents. To avoid opening up the subject about genetic stock, I said, "I don't know why that is." I stood there appearing puzzled, and we moved on to another topic.

My older brother entered a bodybuilding competition in 2006. Watching him stretch and pose, I couldn't help thinking about the links between genes and our behavior. The uniqueness of our bodies, all else being equal (e.g. nutrition, sunlight), is determined solely by our genes. This is analogous to the uniqueness of our personalities. The "great" physique will be predetermined by our genes, however, it is what we do in the environment that molds us and tones us.

Bodybuilding is no different than personality building. We enter the process with predetermined characteristics exclusively set by our genetic soups. It is our clashes with the environment that condition our personalities, just as working out conditions and molds our bodies.

Genes and environment will determine the winners in life, all else being equal. I knew it was highly likely that my brother would win the heavyweight class and the overall competition for all weight classes with ease. It was a no brainer. I just plugged in the variables I knew of him into my loose equation. I knew of no one who has the awesome genetic soup that made up his massive frame, and I knew my brother's disciplined training regimen and drive. That gave me the historical information that led me to pick him as the winner. He was surely a lock for the crown because science doesn't lie, people do. Like many before him, he was just another winner of the genetic lottery.

A lot of who you are was crystallized at the very moment the sperm from your father united with the egg in your mother's womb. These enduring manifestations clash with the environment we will be born into and set us on a crash course in our unique vessels on a constant value chase for what we have deemed valuable in our specific context. We are all unique creatures and must be understood and treated as such. Everything we do is lawful, but not always predictable.

CHAPTER 5 - De-Coding

We cannot escape the fact that our lives are governed by codes. These numerous codes came from many sources and inextricably shape how we act. Our moral, genetic, legal and social codes define our behavioral boundaries, whether we like it or not. Stop and think. What are your codes? How do they shape your behavior? What prevents you from doing one thing or another, or propels you to do it? Many of these questions will be more readily answered upon understanding what drives your behavior. Why did you fight with your friend? What codes of yours were at odds with theirs? We came into this world with our unique codes via genetics and other codes are superimposed on us, creating our reasons for action or inaction.

John Locke, the influential humanist philosopher, believed that the mind of a person at birth was *tabula rasa*, or a blank slate.[1] The more rationalist scientific perspective we now operate with has given that slate some pre-defined characteristics—the templates within which our behavior takes its form.

I would argue that the human body (along with the mind) enters the world with certain preset genetic constants that inevitably affect how we will behave. Our minds may be a blank slate as far as true sensory experience is concerned, but because of genetics we are pre-equipped with certain dispositions that forever influence our behavior. Our minds are littered with pre-charged magnets that idiosyncratically become attracted to different stimuli in the environment—such as sunflower seeds. Who said determinism through genes was dead? Free will is alive and well but may be compromised by strong genetic precursors for deviance or conformity. Genetic determinism does matter because it is a lawful constant in the proof of human behavior. Genes aren't everything, but they are the *main* ingredient in the matrix of human action. This has huge implications as far as criminal justice and other social issues are concerned.

If we could point to strong genetic precursors as a major factor in the actions of a murderer, would that dilute their moral blameworthiness?

Shouldn't their locked-in genetic code be given the benefit of the doubt to dilute their moral blameworthiness, even in the face of free will? Are we truly free? Well, somewhat. Should genetic predispositions be accounted for when sentencing a "guilty" man? This is something to ponder. As my successful, good-looking, muscular, highly intelligent brother once said to me: "It's not my fault I won the genetic lottery." We do have free will, but that free will is shaped by the elements of the genetic vessel we have inherited and by our environment. Blaming certain behaviors on genetics may be valid. However, there is no way to quantify acts that are uniquely influenced by genetics. That is why this issue never enters the equation in determining the guilt or innocence of an accused when it really should—or at least it should have a mitigating effect on their sentence.

Just as the elements that make up our bodies are in lawful order so too are the behaviors that emanate from those elements. We must have a way to manage all of these self-interested behaviors and create some order in our social world. Every populace, through whatever mechanism, makes laws and rules in order to create boundaries to contain people's competing interests at a socially acceptable level. Social codes become concentrated and carried through successive generations through cultural osmosis and generational continuity. Those who govern impose the code onto the people and rule accordingly; in a democratic society, this code is presumably born out of the general will of the people.

Due to our very nature, we must be at the will of a form or system of governance or else, as Hobbes said, we'd all be at war with one another due to our inherently selfish nature. Irrespective of where or how that code is derived, whether it is through a democracy or otherwise, we are all dependent on some system of governance for we could not have peace or order without it. All of us are subservient to the rule of law of our environments. The basic moral codes of cultures around the world have been derived from religion and the consensus of people forged over time.

We all have our interests, and there are many things we would do differently if we were not at the mercy of the law. Laws shape the way people behave by creating certain boundaries and limits within which we may, or may not, indulge in our interests, with punitive consequences for breaches of the law. The governing moral code that governs is very different in different parts of the world because of the consensus of men, which is inextricably linked to culture and religion. In Canada, the consensus of men has determined that it is permissible and legal for an adult to possess and consume alcohol, yet it is a *crime* to possess a marijuana cigarette. The societal harm created by alcohol is so much greater than the societal harm created by marijuana, but we continue to celebrate one and outlaw the other as criminal, which on its face is hypocritical. Yet that is what the consensus of men has determined over the last century. In Saudi Arabia, by contrast, there are strict penalties for alcohol related behavior.

The laws that are imposed on us, wherever we are, inevitably shape our behavior in the contextual realm of the behavioral puzzle. Laws are part of the piece of the behavioral pie that is related to historical context, as I spoke of earlier. These rules and regulations serve to shape our behaviors and may prevent us from doing things we may wish to do, or conversely, make us do things we wouldn't do otherwise. I'm sure we have all broken the law at one time or another. It weighs on our consciences when we break the law. The sense of crossing a boundary has an impact even by its mere thought; even if we don't respect it, we know when we are breaking the code for the most part. We all have our conceptions of justice, based on what we hold to be important. Laws are the simple alliance of value systems, which are really the concentrated values of the consensus of men over time.

I began to consider the weight of the law after an encounter with a couple of individuals late one night. I went down to the local store I had been going to since I was a child, seeking to feed my hunger for sunflower seeds. I pulled up to the store in my brand new BMW and saw a man standing in front of the store eyeballing me like a hungry lion would a gazelle. What he didn't realize was that I was a fox. As soon as I saw him, I knew there was an angle. I said "oh great" to myself as I turned off my car. I knew I was going to hear it the second I got out of my car. What would his story be?

When I got out, he said, "Hey man, I live two hours out of Edmonton and I ran out of gas. I have no money on me to get home. Do you think you could help me out with a few dollars? Anything you could spare would be really appreciated."

Being the concerned citizen that I am, I replied, "Well, how much do you need to get home?"

"Twenty dollars."

"Wow, that's a lot of money," I said. "Well, let me see what I can do."

I opened the front door to the store. As I walked through the store, I noticed that he wasn't alone in this grand scheme. There was another guy outside lurking in the moonlight. They were conversing back and forth outside in front of the store window, and I could see and feel their desperation. Pulling up in my shiny new car, I was a mark immediately. The turbaned man who was working the cash register, who has always called me "Champion" for some reason, said, "Did that guy ask you for money? He's been here for a long time."

"Yes, he did."

I noticed the contempt in his face as he watched them standing outside eyeballing my ride. I was their score, the big fish for that moment, or so they thought. These guys weren't stranded; they were junkies after a hit.

I stalled in the store while the guys waited outside impatiently. Something had to give. I knew it would only be seconds before the inevitable would happen.

The guy who had initially asked me for money walked into the store. He saw me make my purchase and watched how I paid. I was carrying about $500 on me, and paid for my sunflower seeds with a bank card. He walked up behind me and prompted, "So, what's it going to be, man?"

His friend came in next and walked between us, brushing up against me, and looked right into my eyes. He wasn't a pretty sight. He stunk of liquor and his eyes were bloodshot. He had a cleft pallet and looked as if he crawled out of a garbage can.

I looked right into his eyes and gave him my sternest *don't fuck with me* look.

"I'm just passing through," he said, and stood uncomfortably close to me.

My mind was racing. They were losing their patience with me as their next hit loomed somewhere in the future and I was taking my sweet time in the store. Since it was dark outside, I didn't notice the meth marks on the first guy until he'd followed me into the store. In the light of the store, their appearances solidified my early suspicions that they were junkies. To what extent would these guys go to hustle me for some cash? I wasn't about to find out because I like to avoid violent conflicts, being a peace-loving lawyer and all.

I thought, *How can I get out of this situation with the least amount of cost and derive the most benefit?*

I took out a few quarters and dropped them in the first guy's hand. "I'll be right back," I said. I walked out and got in my vehicle swiftly so as to avoid them altogether.

The guy followed me out with his hands in the air yelling, "Hey, where you going?!"

I felt a looming sense of immediate and personal violence. Then I felt an assault on my freedom of movement and my personal space, and I began to feel hostile, too.

When I left, I was enraged. The store I had been coming to for 25 years was now a haven for crack and meth addicts to roam, supporting their addictions at the expense of civil members of the community. It was a slap in the face to me and my community for this to be unfolding here—on *my* turf. Members of the community were being harassed and accosted in order to support the drug habit of two sick people. I couldn't help thinking about all of the people who lived in our neighborhood being exposed to and assaulted by these degenerates. To them, it was all about the next hit, but this was my home, my backyard.

It is one thing to hurt yourself by using drugs, but it's quite another to hurt those around you while on a bender. Those two men had made what was a pleasurable experience for me as a child a completely different experience as an adult. They robbed me of my comfort. They preyed upon the common man with deceit and ill will. This was an affront to social codes in every corner of the globe.

I wanted justice, brutally and directly. I had so much anger in me that I wanted to run them over with my car. My already hot Arab blood reached boiling point. I went a little mad. I wanted to be a vigilante. I couldn't help imposing my moral code on these men. I wanted justice so badly at that very moment. I was starving for it. I wanted justice my way—punishment, swift and severe, as it should be doled out in order for it to be effective, otherwise it rarely works.

It was the law that prevented me from acting in the way I would have liked to that night. They needed help. They were weak. I didn't act. It wasn't worth it to me, even though I was enraged. The costs of beating these guys down and imposing a ban on them panhandling at stores around the neighborhood would have made me feel so good. I would have felt, mentally and physically, that justice was done. I wanted nothing more than to impose my moral code on them in a way that I thought was just. I was at war with them. Our interests collided. They were in direct conflict with me. I wanted to punish them. However, the consensus of men says that I do not have that power by law. Therefore, I could not do what I thought was just. I didn't have the consensus of men on my side. It was too costly for me to get into trouble with these guys. It was the law that stopped me from going back there with a few of my boys, like I used to do in my teens.

It is this consensus that deters many of us from acting one way as opposed to another, and that is one of the principles behind punishments in law. Laws and their corresponding punishments act as deterring mechanisms for people in order to preserve order. By taking conflict out of the hands of enraged individuals and placing it into the cool and sober hands of the state, the preservation of law and order aids and assists us in achieving our interests within the confines of acceptable behavioral boundaries. Without these boundaries, our individual pursuit of self-interest would lead to utter chaos because of the inevitable clashes of man against man in conflicts of interest. Through our reason, we have sought to limit conflict by invoking a higher power, be that government, God, or both, as the source of legal codes.

The imposition of a moral code defines the cocoon of our environment. When the boundaries of the cocoon are breached, the law determines how that breach should best be healed via punishments meted out by the state for the people. This ensures that what we value as a people can be protected, and we may attend to those valuables of interest in a regular, orderly way within the confines of our legal structure.

Acting as individuals, laws will always be breached when an actor has more perceived gain than perceived loss in the face of the law or by mere inadvertence. However, society supersedes the individual, as it forms rules by consensus or through central power that curtails these breaches, via punishment by the law. Justice and punishment is necessary to protect the game of life and to give us the rules by which we play.

Law and order are fluid in the sense that they evolve in order to combat vulnerabilities in the system. These include changing economic conditions, advancements in technology, and more. As our self-interested behaviors change in our pursuit of shifting values, the world we have created around us changes. Not only can our value hierarchy change, but the way we go about satisfying our values can change.

One of the basic human needs is social interaction. Modern life is increasingly defined by interaction through technology. The Internet explosion has forever changed the way people communicate and lead their daily lives. Few could ever foresee the impact the Internet and technology has had on modern society. Personal privacy has come under attack. Information about anything is instantly available to anyone. Faced with such rapid advancements in technology, laws have struggled to keep up and defend against new forms of illegal activity in the world of cyberspace, when such issues were never conceived of prior to the Internet. Laws evolve in tandem with society, redefining the boundaries of what is acceptable even as we push those boundaries ever further.

We operate our lives within certain boundaries that are imposed on us through many different codes that make up who we are and how we act. There is no doubt that the consensus of men shapes our behavior through laws and punishments. It is via our genetic, moral, social, legal and instinctual codes that our behaviors are forged and play out in a multitude of ways. Our decision to act one way as opposed to another always comes into play when we act in the real world, because of the recipe of codes that govern us.

Should I? Or shouldn't I? Those are the questions we continually ask ourselves, being the rough economists that we are. It is all about weighing the relative strengths of the codes via what is valuable to us to determine how we will act in a given situation. Our genetic code *always* remains part of this process. However, the weight given to it in our decision-making process is already built in. Our geneavior always has say in every decision we make no matter what. We process environmental information through our genetic sieve idiosyncratically, and thereby act one way or another. Thus, we are mere actors superimposed with codes derived from nature and our contexts. The commingling of these codes can be used to predict what we will do next and where we will take ourselves. Knowing that these codes are our vehicles for action uncovers why we do what we do.

CHAPTER 6 - Reinforcement and Equilibrium

From an early age, we are able to understand what actions will bring us pleasure and what actions will bring us harm. Through watching and through trial and error, we learn. We learn as we collide with the environment awaiting us, from the moment we exit the womb with all of our characteristics predetermined by genetic variance. We are learning almost every second as we tread through the external world. Learning is simply finding out what we perceive or deem as valuable, and we continually pursue that value. Value is determined by genetics, reinforcement (in our environment), and symbolism.

In relation to our interactions with the environment, we are constantly seeking value, whatever that symbolically means to us at that point in our lives. As stated, Freud would contend that a great majority of our behaviors are geared toward tension reduction. Tension reduction, from a physiological point of view, is just one variable in the equation. Tension reduction is analogous to negative reinforcement. Negative reinforcement is the removal of a negative stimulus that makes people more likely to behave in such a way toward a negative stimulus so as to remove its affects because it has negative value.

However, people behave in certain ways when there is no tension at all, as with positive reinforcement. Committing a behavior that has been positively reinforced in the past brings us something of value. We believe a certain behavior is valuable when it has removed a negative stimulus or brought us a positive gain. This makes the behaviors which attained these valuables more likely to occur in the future when we face similar contextual situations. These behaviors will be committed in order to satisfy our self-interest. It is when behavior achieves value that makes it more likely to occur in the future, because we are all value chasers.

I was sitting in sentencing class in my last year of law school, and we were talking about the principles behind sentencing criminals, including deterrence, denunciation, and retribution. We were on the topic of crime and punishment when the professor asked, "Why is it that criminals will still continue to commit crimes at approximately the same rate, even when stiffer penalties are enacted in the hopes that the criminal would be more hesitant in the face of a more severe penalty such as the death penalty?" The professor suggested that the criminal might be oblivious as to what the punishment will be, and therefore the punishment doesn't serve as a deterrent. He suggested that criminals may also fail to see the consequences of their actions, and just do what they like and hope they get away with it.

I pondered this little conversation we were having. Almost every criminal act done by any individual arouses that person's conscience, unless they are a complete psychopath or so mentally unfit that they really have no concept of right and wrong. They know that there is a negative consequence, but the *perceived* negative consequence is a minimal cost compared to what the perceived benefit is, and that is why the criminal continues to do what he does. They know there is a negative consequence that is proportional in severity to their criminal act. It is about pros and cons (no pun intended). However, not every pro and con carries the same value or cost for every actor.

The power of perception is closely tied to the power of reinforcement. If one sees another person being punished for a particular behavior, the likelihood of the observer acting in the same way as the punished person will be diminished. This is unless the perceived self-interest of the observer supersedes the perceived punishment or response cost of the behavior. Even more, as these two things (perception and reinforcement) are working in conjunction, we almost become slaves to our environments because of what we perceive will happen next and the behavioral model we find ourselves in.

As I do many real estate deals for people, I hold a lot of people's money in a trust account. My account gets up into the millions at times. A lot of people joke with me and say that I should grab that money and take off to Mexico or somewhere warm, where I'll live happily ever after. Believe it or not, a few lawyers have done this in their time. However, would I do something like that? Probably not. That's because I would be disbarred and sitting in a jail cell for at least a few years, pondering what to do with all that money I hid in a safe place.

In other words, I see costs to this action: I'd lose the respect of my peers. I'd be seen as a rogue by many people I care about. I am impacted by those people and care how they see me and how I look at myself and feel about myself. The stolen money wouldn't be as enjoyable nor as deserved as earned money. I would lose the respect of my huge family, whom I care deeply about. I would shame my parents and my brothers, and so on and so forth. So, the cost of illegality to me would be immense. But would I do it for $5 billion? A lot of lawyers would drop off the face of the earth given such an opportunity.

Considering reinforcement, if a lawyer was already a millionaire, having another couple of million by taking money that didn't belong to him wouldn't really change his life all that much. However, the comparative costs would be great. Even money has diminishing reinforcement value. The reason some lawyers can be bought and would disappear is due to the fact that they don't care how people see them as long as they have money. They would have 10 million reasons to disregard everybody else. That is why it has been done before, and it will happen again.

Some lawyers get themselves into a situation and environment where the perceived benefits of taking the money actually outweigh the perceived costs. Picture a lawyer with a drug addiction, a messy divorce, a dwindling practice, and a failing reputation. That is your candidate. Many lawyers actually get disbarred for stealing clients' trust funds to feed their drug habits or other addictions in the hopes that they will put the money back before anyone knew what happened. They are so deep into their addictions that they no longer connect the rules to their own situation. The perceived costs are outweighed by the perceived benefits. Consequence has little weight in the cost-benefit analysis carried out in the mind of the trust fund bilking lawyer.

I sit at my desk and I hesitate about what to write here because what I am about to tell you is something very powerful and useful. I could literally write a book just on this subject alone and give countless examples of how your behavior and the behavior of others is not so much just the unraveling of human behavior exclusive of any inputs or outputs. The reason this chapter is so important is because it is the one most useful to us in the real world. In order to explain behavior, one must study it closely and extensively. I've spent the past 15 years observing and studying people out of a yearning to know the truth about behavior.

There are certain schedules of reinforcement that can allow us to manipulate features of our surroundings to assist us in our pursuit of self-interest. When an actor behaves in a certain way and receives something that has value to him or her, the likelihood of the actor behaving in that way again increases. This is because we are creatures of self interest, after all. So, when you get something you perceive as being valuable for a behavior you have committed, it makes the behavior more likely to occur in the future. That something of value is called a reinforcer. The reinforcer supports the behavior so as to make it more likely that the behavior will be committed again, as long as the actor desires that particular reinforcer.

There have been countless examples of experiments showing that a mouse that makes the connection between pressing a lever and getting a food pellet will press that lever when it is hungry: the food serves as the reinforcer. It makes the behavior of pushing the lever more likely because it has reinforcing power due to the resulting value obtained by the mouse.

If every one time the mouse presses that lever, one food pellet comes out, we call that a fixed schedule of reinforcement—the mouse is reinforced *once* for every *one* lever press. This places the behavior at the level of FSR1—that is a Fixed Schedule of Reinforcement, with one response required to receive a reinforcer. Fixed schedules of reinforcement are set at a certain point, and once the actor is reinforced a few times on that schedule, they learn the pattern. They learn that they will be reinforced every time after a given number of specific responses, however many that may be. If a pellet were to come out on every fourth press of the lever, then that would still be a fixed schedule of reinforcement as well, because the subject being reinforced for performing a certain behavior must perform it four times to get something of reinforcing value. This scenario would be at the level of FSR4, meaning that the reinforcing event will only come to fruition if the behavior to bring it about is done four times.

What is so powerful about schedules of reinforcement is that they apply to humans as well. However, it is the power of the *variable* schedule of reinforcement that is the key here, not the fixed variety. Now that you understand what a fixed schedule of reinforcement is, let's get acquainted with how a variable schedule of reinforcement works, because that is the schedule of reinforcement with the most power over the actor.

When someone is on a variable schedule of reinforcement, the number of responses required to bring about the positive (or negative) reinforcer varies from trial to trial. The number of responses needed in order to bring about the reinforcer, food for example, is a random number. The actor never knows how many responses it will take until he is reinforced. However, having received something of value once, he or she will continue to act in the same way in the hope of being rewarded again. The actor comes to make the connection and thinks that he will most likely be reinforced from time to time as long as he continues to commit the previous behavior that was reinforced the first time.

I will give a few examples to make sure that this is crystal clear in your mind. A mouse could be put on a variable schedule of reinforcement with a positive reinforcer of food. This means that the number of times that the mouse will have to press the lever for food to be reinforced (get food) will vary (hence the term variable) every time the mouse is reinforced. The mouse could press the lever just twice and get a food pellet. The next time it could be 22 times before it gets a pellet. The next time could be eight times, and the time after that could be five, one, nine, 31, and so on.

What is so amazing about this is that if we set the level of reinforcement at 40 responses before the mouse is reinforced, that mouse will continue to pound away at that lever, especially if it is hungry and has already been reinforced a number of times previously. The mouse doesn't know just when it will come, but acts as though its next hit (food) is just around the corner.

This is the most powerful schedule of reinforcement, as a means of eliciting the greatest number of responses. There have been thousands of controlled experiments confirming this phenomenon for all of you empiricists out there. It is as if the mouse gets hooked on playing or pressing. The mouse becomes a lever pressing junkie as long as it remains hungry, but food will lose its reinforcing value as the mouse gets full.

This compulsion to behave in a continuous way with such vigor doesn't occur in the fixed schedule of reinforcement, nor does it in the two other schedules of reinforcement that are set by time (fixed and variable times). It is only the variable response schedule that produces what I call the "junkie effect." The other schedules produce other response gradients related to the schedule of reinforcement the subject finds him or herself in. I discuss the variable schedule because it has the most power over the actor or value seeker. Enough talking about mice, because I can already feel the criticism of those of you out there who think studying animals to learn the behavior of humans is frivolous, invalid, and unreliable.

Let's use a real life example, with real people. Blackjack. I'm sure most of you have been in a situation where you are watching someone gamble and they just won't leave the table. Why is that? It is because they are sitting on a table where the schedule of reinforcement is variable. When that blackjack player puts that money on the table, there is no guarantee that he or she will be reinforced with a winning hand and money to follow.

Let's say a player wagered a bet on blackjack and on the first hand he won. He lost the second, third and fourth hands and won the fifth. I think you can see where this is going. Because the player is on a variable schedule of reinforcement—he is being rewarded, or winning, at completely unpredictable and random times of placing a bet—he is vulnerable to losing a lot of money. He will keep on plunking those chips down thinking it will be a winner this time—and maybe it will be. This schedule is very powerful at making people perform many stereotypical behaviors over and over, thinking that because they were reinforced in the past, they will be reinforced in the future at some point. However, a player loses sight of the fact that chasing that reinforcer, like a mouse would chase a food pellet, may be more costly in the long run because the odds favor the house. Before he knows it, he is hooked on playing, just like the mouse was on the lever. This is how the gambling junkie is created.

The same principles apply to a slot machine. We find ourselves pulling that lever time after time in the hunt for that reinforcer coming at random times. Like the mouse, we may become lever-pressing junkies, which can become dangerous to our lives if carried on unchecked over time. Knowing the science behind why we exhibit these behaviors will undoubtedly allow us to have a moment of self-reflection and understanding as we catch ourselves in the abyss of a dangerous variable schedule of reinforcement. By having a deeper understanding of what is going on, we may take action and stop or seek intervention.

The "junkie effect" is very, very powerful. When you hit, it gives you a rush. It's euphoric, but it is dangerous. You can use it to your advantage and make people behave in all sorts of ways. For those who get addicted to this behavior pattern (I mean out-of-control gambling), I truly feel bad for you. There is nothing worse than a gambling degenerate. I have little sympathy for someone who gets hooked into this pattern of behavior and allows it to destroy his or her life.

Whyology

I was once overcome by the effect of the variable schedule of reinforcement. My deadly game was roulette. There are 38 slots (including 0 and 00) on the wheel, and players more or less place chips on a table with numbers where they think the ball will stop on the wheel. I was in my third year of university, and I had taken the bus to the mega mall about 20 blocks from my house. It was winter, so I wasn't about to walk home. I just missed my bus home, and the next one wasn't due for another 40 minutes. So, to kill time, I thought I'd make a brief trip to the casino in the mall. I walked in, and I immediately knew that roulette would be my game.

A player's fate is decided quite quickly with roulette, so it fit well with my schedule. I cashed in $60 and let it ride. I made a good hit. I still remember it was one of my favorite numbers: 29 hit. If you play a number straight up, a winner pays 35 to one. So, for every one chip bet on the number, you would receive 35 in return if the ball landed on your number.

I started with four dollars on it, and now I had $140 plus my original stake. I missed the next spin and the next. I was out of money. My original $60 evaporated in front of my eyes over three spins of the wheel. I felt that burning anger that you get when you lose fast in the casino. I'm sure a lot of you know what I am talking about. Luckily, I had my bank card on me. I went to the ATM and took out $100. I played it all in one spin, and I lost. I went back again and got another $100. I played the whole $100 on a spin. I hit it hard this time—"Yes!" It was the other monster number that I loved to play: number 31. That time, I had bet eight straight up, which paid me 280 chips in return. I had stacks in front of me, and I began to collect some onlookers behind me. I felt an awesome rush come through me like a shot of pure adrenalin into my veins. I was high on dopamine and felt pure euphoria. Nothing I had ever done felt so good to me.

Five spins later, I was broke again. Sweating and trying to quell my racing heart, I went to the bank machine once again. I was mindless; irrational. Money had no value to me. I was in a trance. I took out $200, and I lost it in two spins. I went back and forth for two hours until my bank account was drained and I maxed out my Visa. I lost close to $5,000 in that two-hour span.

I left the casino with $50 in my pocket and an ill feeling in my stomach. I was numb and literally in shock. I was like a robot at that table. I had no control of myself for two hours. That is a scary thought. I jumped in a taxi waiting just outside the casino doors. When the taxi stopped at my house, the fare was about eight dollars. I remember telling the taxi driver what I had done, and I gave him the whole $50. Yes, that's right; I tipped him about $42. I remember telling him that I didn't deserve the money. It was worth more than $42 to me to give that money to the taxi driver than it was to keep it because of how I felt about myself. Not in the taxi driver's wildest dreams did he think that on the way to my house, which is a quick ride in a car, would I tip him $42. However, as he gained more historical context and saw how upset I was and how I hated myself for losing control, it wasn't such a shock when I told him to keep it. It made some sense to him after he learned of my unfortunate night. It was in my interest to give him the money because not having any money made me feel better than having just $42 in my pocket. There was value to me in giving the money away. Get it?

Most of the worst gamblers I know have hit it big a few times in the casino, which makes their addiction all that much stronger. They are in a *variable schedule* environment coupled with the fact that they can perceive themselves walking out of the casino with a big roll of money in their pockets, drawing on a memory of their last big score. They feel that they can win big because history doesn't lie. The junkie effect of the gambler is intensified because of deeply held beliefs or perceptions that they are just one hand away from a major run that will send them walking out of the casino with bags full of money.

After that incident, I refused to ever become that robot again. I knew that I was highly susceptible and predisposed to games of chance, especially because of how good I felt psychologically and physiologically when I hit the jackpot. It is just as addictive as heroin; and it brings similar feelings of euphoria with it as well. I fought it off, and I won. I could never be in that place again because I wasn't in control. Once you lose control, you are purely at the mercy of your environment and those around you. Don't be a slave to your external world with no power to leave, stop, or say no. Understand what is propelling your behavior. Save yourself from your awful behaviors, see what's going on, and know what is making you do these things psychologically.

I made a contract with myself that I would never allow myself to be in that position ever again. This contract was buoyed by something very important to me, and I stuck with it. I placed very high value on the contract so as not to break it. We all have our own highly valuable things that we cherish, and using knowledge of these things as a starting point will be of great assistance to you. By sheer force of will, I made a strict and powerful promise to myself that this would never happen again. Nothing brought me that feeling of utter exhilaration that gambling did. It was intoxicating. With that in mind, I knew I needed to stop because it was a dangerous behavior that was extremely rewarding to me simply because of my genetic predisposition. In order to want to change, we have to want to change from within first. If we don't, nothing and nobody will be of any assistance because we will inevitably find ourselves back in the same dangerous places behaving in the same dangerous ways.

A couple of weeks later, I entered a casino and watched my friends play blackjack. It was rewarding to me to stand and watch and muster up the will to abstain from my vice. It takes will and courage to stop anything that brings us dangerous euphoria. That night of roulette was a blessing in disguise. My story shows the power of variable reinforcement in causing me to think that I would win big on the next spin. The environment had full control over me. I behaved like a classic junkie. I was on a variable schedule of reinforcement—I even knew the science behind it, and it got me. I wouldn't let it happen again, though. If someone who is as knowledgeable about psychology as I am can let that happen, then it can happen to almost anyone. It takes guts to know that you are susceptible and to walk away from the table or any vice you have. It was rewarding to stand in front of a table and not play. It made me feel good to know that I was in control.

I've seen many gamblers in my life, and I have pleaded with one in particular to stop, but it was too late for him. He had been gambling for years when I gave him a talk. The power of the variable schedule of reinforcement had him so deep in that he couldn't move. He is over 50 now, and I think he has finally slowed down after 25 years of out-of-control gambling. An extreme addiction to gambling—or anything, for that matter—makes us compromise our shame for that next hit. The power of "it" makes some lie to loved ones, steal from anyone close by, and do things that they wouldn't normally do. I call it "the fever." When someone chases off out of control after something, I say, "That guy has the fever." It is that delirious state you get in when you want something really, really badly—like another hit of drugs, or another spin at the roulette wheel. It is when you'll do almost anything to be able to get that next hit, thinking, "It will come. It will come. Just once more."

The same reasoning also applies to all of the crack junkies out there. One of the reasons that crack is so addictive is that the vast majority of the users are on a variable schedule of reinforcement. Not only do the hits of crack they use vary in their potency and ability to get them high, but the quest for the drug is an adventure on its own schedule of reinforcement. For users, the first high may have been really good, while the second was not as good. Maybe the third time was better than the second, and the fourth and fifth time were a bust because the rock turned out to be candle wax. This is not a variable schedule of reinforcement per se because there is reinforcing value most of the time. However, the reinforcing effects are so variable that it is akin to getting a push (a tie) with the dealer at a blackjack table. It isn't bad, but it isn't that good either. This doesn't apply to all drugs, because most drugs are physiologically addicting, and people want to do them because of the other side of reinforcement: negative reinforcement.

As I have stressed in the forgoing, both positive and negative reinforcement make the behavior that brought about the reinforcement in the first place more likely in the future. In positive reinforcement, we get a positive stimulus (something of value) for our behavior, thus making that behavior, or series of behaviors, more likely in the future. In negative reinforcement, we are removing a negative stimulus with our behavior, also making the behavior more likely in the future. An example of negative reinforcement is taking an aspirin when you have a headache. It is reinforcing because you are removing a negative stimulus (the headache) by doing the behavior (taking an aspirin), thus making it more likely that you will take an aspirin for a headache the next time around.

Many people are addicted to drugs because they are in a cycle of negative reinforcement. This is evident in the case of someone who regularly uses heroin and becomes physiologically addicted to it. The regular user will have severe withdrawal if they stop using. In order to get rid of this withdrawal, he or she must use again to stop the body from overcompensating in the opposite way to the drugs effect. For example, taking opiates such as morphine, codeine, or heroin causes constipation in people. The body attempts to compensate for this constipation. It becomes conditioned to deal with the constipation by an equilibrium action of loosening the bowels. When the drug wears off, and the next day rolls around, the body is still in that conditioned phase and the user now has diarrhea and other withdrawal symptoms. The one sure way to get rid of these is to use again. It is the removal of all of the negative stimuli associated with withdrawal that makes the user indulge. It is simply negative reinforcement: removing a negative stimulus (diarrhea) with behavior (using heroin), thus making the behavior more likely in the future.

It is a double whammy with drugs, because not only do you get negative reinforcement from getting rid of those nasty withdrawals, you also get some positive reinforcement from the euphoric feeling of the drugs. Of course, every turn of the cycle digs the user one foot deeper into the black abyss. The next withdrawal will be worse and the next high will be smaller. That is why an addict will most likely use again—for both positive and negative reinforcement. It is done in the pursuit of reinforcement. The same goes for cocaine and other drugs that have powerful effects on human physiology. Gambling also has an effect on the pleasure center in people's brains.

If you are still skeptical about variable schedules of reinforcement, I will let you in on something that will change the way people communicate (or don't communicate) forever. I bet there are a few of you out there who already do this, but once the masses find out about it, there are going to be a lot of broken phones out there. It involves using a variable schedule of reinforcement on your significant, or not-so-significant, other. It will drive him or her absolutely up the wall, but he or she will value every second that they are reinforced. Are you there yet? Do you know where I am going with this? You might. Here is how the experiment goes: if you have been seeing a girl or guy for a while, and you want that person to really value talking to you more and to feel a greater feeling of reinforcement when he or she does talk to you, put them on a variable schedule of reinforcement. Next time he/she calls, screen the call. Just don't answer it. See if he or she calls back a second time.

A little historical context is also needed for this. If your date is known to call back when you don't pick up the first time, then chances are he or she will call back a second time, too, but maybe at a later time. By screening the person's calls and answering the phone after a random number of calls, instead of every time they call, you will convert them from a schedule that was akin to a fixed schedule or FSR1 (that is, you answer the phone every time they call), to a variable schedule of reinforcement, where you only answer after a random number of calls chosen by you. Maybe you answer after the third call on Wednesday, on the first on Thursday, on the second call on Saturday. Sunday you were too hung over, and you answered after the seventh call. By now he\she is becoming just like the mouse in the cage or the gambler on the roulette table. The behavior is the phone call and the positive stimulus (or reinforcer) is you answering and the caller hearing your voice. You have the person who is calling thinking, *she has to answer this time.* You have just created the junkie effect with your significant other as the test subject. Shame on you! Is it in your interest to have so much attention? If done correctly, you will have your caller pressing those buttons on his or her phone so many times the caller will need more fingers. When you do answer, it will be so rewarding to the caller. This will work as long as the caller places value on having you answer the phone— which of course he does, or else he wouldn't be calling you in the first place. You may get bawled out, but remember: you are in control here. This is your experiment. Your voice will sound better to the caller, and you may get an earful, but honestly, he or she will be really happy to be talking to you. Remember, though, that everyone has a burnout point or extinction point. What that point is can only be known by the caller, but the receiver of the calls will have a good idea of what his or her call patterns are just from historical context of the relationship.

There are countless other ways that this can be used to your benefit by increasing the response patterns in people, but I think giving you a framework to work from is good enough for now. I don't want to create too many mad scientists out there. It's just science. We were meant to discover these phenomena. Putting someone on a variable schedule like this should not be used if you have a great relationship. If you like where you're at, then don't go there. This is just something to try for those of you who need some techniques to make that person out there value you a bit more.

I tell people to make themselves a commodity: make yourself a little scarcer. Your partner will value you more for it. Some alone time is good for everyone, but not too much because the key is balance. If you have been too available, and it seems the ease of your availability has been taken for granted, you may want to convert to a variable schedule for a while. Being too available and always ready when your partner, or anyone else, needs you makes conditions ripe for him or her to take advantage of you, which unfortunately happens all of the time. It is kind of like the saying, "Familiarity breeds contempt." A guy who is too readily in his woman's face and always *there* will get it sooner or later, and vice versa. Just as I said earlier, there has to be balance: too much of anything is no good.

Whyology

Likewise, when a man perceives that his lady will just "be there" all of the time waiting for him, he may take it for granted and take advantage of the situation. I remember telling a girl about this one day when the conversation turned to the fact that her boyfriend wasn't calling her that often. I explained this method to her, and she thought I was a little crazy at first. I never saw her again after that, and I still wonder if she tried it. I'd really like to run into her one day just to ask her. I assured her it would work as long as the person calling had enough interest in talking to her.

Not long ago one of my best friends called me up and said he had found this girl's number in his phone and couldn't remember for the life of him who she was. His inability to remember may have been related to the fact that he had consumed many drinks just prior to entering her number in his cell phone. He told me that he texted her, and she texted him back asking who it was. He just didn't want to come out and say his name because he didn't know whom he would be telling. He texted her back, and she texted him back three times, and he still had not responded with a name. His question to me was, "What should I write now? Or should I say anything at all?"

I asked him when the last time she responded was. He said, "About 20 minutes ago," and he hadn't responded to any of the last three texts. Well, she was probably done trying to get a response because my friend had put her on a schedule of extinction, meaning that no matter how many responses are given there will be no reinforcement. Her extinction point was low because of the unfamiliar relationship that they had. This meant she would eventually cease her behavior (texting) because she was not being reinforced. So, he asked me if he should send a text back to her because he wanted to find out who she was. My answer was, "Oh, you have to. If it has been 20 minutes since you last wrote anything, she most likely has put you out of her mind for the time being." In order to keep the variable sequence going, she needed to have something sent to her that had a little bit of reinforcing value—something to pique her curiosity. This would help elicit the desired response from her again and get her back on a reinforcing schedule. I know it sounds a little perverse—but science isn't always pretty (a statement Albert Einstein would have agreed with).

If he wanted to find out who she was—which he did—he had to text her back. So he did, and, lo and behold, the texting took off from there. By the time I drove to his house—about 10 minutes away—he knew

80

exactly who she was, where she worked, and that she was sitting with her pissed-off boyfriend.

I always get phone calls from people asking me what to do in their relationships—what move to make next or how to react to a certain situation. I feel more like a marriage counselor than a lawyer sometimes. I always get these types of calls from clients and from friends. They know I usually have a psychological curveball ready for most situations.

I was driving downtown with a friend, and he was talking about the way that I am with people and about my intuition. He called me the weirdest but most fitting thing: he called me a "wizard." I had never been called that before, but I knew what he meant. He knew that I know the score most of the time in most situations. I know what is on people's minds, and I know what people (most of them, anyway) are doing, and saying, and *why*. Maybe that's why I'm a good poker player. I explained to him, as I always do, that I was a behavioral psychology prodigy. As soon as he said that, I swore that I was going to put it in this book. I am a wizard, but only a wizard at behavioral psychology. I am just average at all the other subjects.

My advice to most people comes from a position of simplicity and balance. By looking at a situation objectively as possible, we can piece together what interests are at odds between parties. With this in mind, only then can we make proper solutions.

The schedules of reinforcement are constantly at work in our daily lives. By understanding which schedules and reinforcers are at play, we may be able to divert ourselves or a loved one from the abyss of a dangerous behavioral pattern such as gambling. Stop and think of all the things that bring you value in a day and how your actions are involved. From using the ATM, to going through a drive through window, we are being reinforced by our actions on schedules of reinforcement. Observe your own behavior and make the connections. You will see your life in a new light.

CHAPTER 7 - Perception

The way we behave in the world has a lot to do with how we perceive the world, past and present, and how we want to represent ourselves among the others that surround us. We all see the world differently because we have all had differing experiences and we all have different genes to filter them. No two people will ever "see" the same thing for what it really is because we all have different historical contexts and we idiosyncratically look through our genetic "goggles" to perceive things in different ways. It's not as straightforward as the perceptions of colors and hues. We give value to our own perceptions of the world and what we believe to be true.

What we make others perceive to be "true" has profound effects on how others respond to us. Everybody has insecurities in their lives. A person's level of insecurity can be placed on a continuum from a lot to a little. Our insecurities come from many sources, be it our weight, height, looks, age, lack of success, and more.

People act in certain ways, knowing how they understand the world to be, in order to make others perceive them in a certain light in the service of their self-interest. Think of your neighbor who is financed to the neck, drives a shiny new car, lives in the biggest house on the block, but doesn't have a penny in the bank. You might perceive him to have the good life. However, that life exists as an outer shell only, with nothing holding it up on the inside. Your neighbor has a real interest in the way he is perceived by others. Thus, he takes steps to ensure that he is looked upon in a favorable light, possibly to conceal what he lacks. Our self-interest governs how we would like to be perceived by others and sets out the steps we take to make others perceive us in a certain way. There are those who don't care what others think because they give no or little value to the opinions of others, but these few are the exception not the rule.

I often hear people say to each other, "You're weird." I was eating lunch the other day with one of my lawyer friends and our receptionist. I started off on one of my tangents, and our receptionist said, "You're weird."

"How am I weird?" I asked.

"You just are."

"How?" I responded. "Explain yourself."

"I can't. I just can't put it into words."

Another guy that worked at the office was also with us. He looked at her and said, "What is 'weird,' anyway?"

Nothing and nobody is "weird." Weird is just a term that means what another sees in you is incongruent with what they believe is "normal." But we are all different because we all have different genes and experiences. So, relative to each other, we are all a little weird. Weird is a relative term: it is what one thinks is different based on what he or she perceives to be usual or customary in *their* world. If someone perceives what you do as "abnormal," then you're weird.

The beauty of being weird is that there are so many different people in the world with different ways of dressing, speaking, eating and so on. Weird is the spice of life. The more egocentric and rigid we are, the weirder we will think others are. This is because we overvalue our view of the way things should be and the status quo of our surroundings, friends, culture, and so on. This is the root of racism and prejudice. The more different someone appears to be from us, the more likely we will see them in a contrasting light. Sometimes that light has racist or prejudicial underpinnings. It is perception that is key here.

Of course, there are things that are truly so deviant that they go beyond "weird," such as the compulsions of a murderer or a pedophile. Their behavior would be weird but understandable if you break it down because all behavior can be explained; no matter how sick and demented something may be, it all has some kind of explanation. All behavior is lawful, but not necessarily predictable. All of our actions are governed by the same set of principled laws that drive us to do certain things based on the coupling of our genetic soups and our previous historical interactions with the environment.

Whyology

When I was in law school I'd see this guy with a huge Mohawk hairdo in the parking lot at school. I'd think to myself, on a behavioral scientific level, *why would he do that?* I knew there was a reason because there is a purpose for every action that we consciously commit in the environment. There could be a multitude of reasons. I initially thought that this guy was weird. But was he? Maybe he thought I was weird for wearing a sheepskin jacket with a fur collar and designer jeans.

We may have thought that about each other because of differing points of reference. That is why historical context matters. It is the mosaic of all of our interactions in the environment that lays the foundation in our minds for the way things are and should be. It is the cluster of cause and effect events that has brought us to a certain point in time to see the world in a particular light. Underlying all of this is the constant in the equation of human behavior, which is our genetic soup. If I asked 10 people that know you well to describe you, there would be a general consensus on certain behavioral traits that forms part of your core self. These are almost strictly derived from the variations in our genetic codes. We are each an idiosyncratic beast that collides with the physical world via our five senses. This is what makes us all weird. We are who we are—but how can we change?

I have always thought about people's hairdos, or lack of them, as a reflection of who they are. Why do you do your hair the way you do it? I remember seeing that guy with the towering Mohawk. I couldn't help but wonder *why* in the hell anybody would waste their time getting up in the morning and dealing with that jazz—but of course there's a reason. There always is.

People shape their hair in a certain way because that is how they want to be perceived by the outside world. They want to take over the observers' eyes and see themselves as they would like to be seen. That spiky hairdo may be serving many functions at one time—self-expression, rebellion, conformity to a certain peer group, being noticed, freedom, uniqueness, etc. However, it remains a display for the many onlookers and observers. When we get our hair cut, dyed, colored, styled, lengthened, it is for onlookers as much as for ourselves. We have them in our minds when we flip through a style magazine and take a seat in the stylist's chair. Sure, it makes us feel good, but it is as much for the actor as it is for whom the actor wishes to cross paths with. What will x or y think of this? How will I

Whyology

feel about this? Can I deal with what people will think or say to me? How will the average Joe see me with this new hairdo? The actor tries to live out what he wants others to believe of him, good or bad.

I have some grey hairs on my head that have been multiplying by the week. I recently went to a barber friend of mine who put me in the chair and immediately began to dye my hair. Why in the hell would he do such a thing, especially without me asking for it? Well, he had the dye sitting there from the previous client and the rest was going to be thrown out anyway. Financially, it was in his interest to put the dye on my hair. It would double what I was going to pay him and stretch his supplies twice as far in one slap of the dye brush. He thought it would be in my interest to have my hair dyed because I had recently turned 30 years old and had a lot of grey hairs for my age. Otherwise, I looked about 25. At the time, I had been growing my hair out for the first time in a decade. Since then, many people have told me that my new do looks "awesome." I have never been complimented so much on my hair in my life, greys and all. I ask others if I should dye my hair, and the overwhelming response is "No!"

At times I wear a suit to work, and unfortunately I am in a profession where it pays to look as old as you can. I had a little bit of a chubby face and the longer hair was more proportionate with my face and head. Many have said that I look distinguished with the greys and the longer hairdo, especially when I'm wearing a suit. I get more respect from other lawyers. Clients seem to have more faith in me. Judges seem to listen to me more. Many more people call me "Sir." (Well, I don't think that's a good thing since I still feel like a teenager.) People's perception of me with the longer hair is more "lawyer-like" for some reason, and it has actually been good for business. It has become increasingly valuable for me to continue to grow my hair. The reaction was unexpected, almost bizarre. I couldn't believe the power a simple change of hairdo could have. Was it because strangers' perception of me had changed? Or, have I created a new persona to project through my greys?

If there is one thing you should take from this anecdote, it's that if you want people to see you in a way that may be advantageous in your life, doing something as simple as changing your hairstyle may have profound effects on how you are seen and how people deal with you. Pick a hairstyle that compliments the structure and contours of your face. The length and style of your hair can have profound effects on how you are observed by others in a multitude of ways and in turn make you feel good about yourself—and that's good, because it's all about you.

The first piece of advice I have for you has to do with your appearance. A few small changes to the way you dress and groom yourself can have profound effects with the ladies or men out there and with the way that others view you in all kinds of social and business relationships. We could all clean up a little and dress, smell, and look better for our female (or male) counterparts and for others in society generally. Personal appearance can have profound effects on one's life and can change the way people interact with you and approach you.

There have been countless studies on the way people with different appearances have been treated in the same controlled environment. In these experiments, appearance serves as the independent variable, which is the thing that is changed or altered in an experimental study. Researchers dressed one way or another and went into the exact same place, and how they were treated varied based on their appearance. Those dressed "classier" were generally treated better and more favorably than those dressed unattractively. This is what would be called the response or the dependent variable. The response was correlated with appearance.[1]

Our appearance should be kept in order. It takes a lot of work to keep that appearance looking fresh but it is so important to look good and feel good about yourself. The self-image you portray to the world should be fine-tuned before you even walk out the door in the morning, even before you have a particular girl in mind that you would like to court. Knowing you are at your best makes you more confident and makes others more attracted to you. Confidence goes a long way, and it is bolstered by how we feel we appear to the world and by how others perceive us.

Being a lawyer working downtown, I must wear a suit when I attend court. Every time I go downtown in jeans, guys I know from law school give me a hard time. So I try to wear a suit to work—even though I hate wearing a suit. I do notice something, though. When I wear a suit, I am treated much differently by the public than when I am wearing a dress shirt and a pair of jeans. When I have a "fly" suit on, people call me "Sir." People on the street corner waiting for the cross light warm up to me. When I walk behind a woman on a street downtown, I know she is completely at ease because I have my suit on. When I go to make a deposit at the bank and all of the bankers and tellers see me, the response I receive from them is greater than the one I get when I go in jeans. Wearing the uniform, I belong. It's a fact of life that appearance and attire have a profound effect on the way we are treated and viewed by others around us.

The next step is health, where the changes move from the inside to the outside. To begin looking a little healthier, try some exercise, including some cardio to get the blood flowing in your body and to help you look a little more chiseled in the face. For those of you who hate weights or the monotony of the gym (like me), it is a good idea to try something more fun, such as tennis or hockey. I once bought a membership at a gym not far from my house. I remember I was paying about $45.00 per month. I was all gung ho about getting in great shape and looking like someone on a magazine cover. In 18 months, I think I went to the gym twice. I couldn't stand the place. I couldn't stand the monotony of lifting heavy weights and putting them back down or running nowhere on a treadmill. Looking back, I paid over $400.00 per workout! However, I played hockey with my friends and cousins just about every weekend, which kept me in pretty good shape. The gym is not for everyone, just like school is not for everyone. However, if you don't have an education, you better have something else on the go and if you are not a regular member at a gym, you'd better be doing something to get that heart rate going. It will be worth it, so just do it.

Another important thing here is diet. It is easy to make a few changes that will improve your health and caloric intake in positive ways. Stay away from all white powders when it comes to food. These are things such as sugar, flour, and salt. Sugar that is not used by your body is converted into fat and is stored somewhere, usually where you don't want it. Salt is bad for your kidneys and makes your face look bloated, taking away from your good looks. Instead of drinking pop or juice, drink water—this will be a good head start on the way to having you feel and look better. Obesity is a huge problem today, and a few simple life changes such as cutting cola out of your diet can have profound effects. You should eat like a caveman, with a diet rich in fruits, vegetables, and meats. Dairy is okay in moderation. A good dose of multi-grains is good, too. This is not a diet or nutrition book, but these little tips can go a long way. These little tips will improve your life and the way you are treated and perceived by those around you. The more people perceive you in a favorable light, the more favorably you will be treated and the better your life will be.

Whyology

When you first start dating someone, you want to be perceived in a certain light. You'll go to absurd lengths to have yourself perceived a certain way, especially if you have an idea of what type of mate your date likes. I have a cousin who took a girl out, knowing from her friends that she liked guys who were dangerous and up to no good: the classic bad boy. My cousin fashioned himself into a mysterious gangster type by wearing his leather jacket, slicking his hair, listening to gangster music, and getting random phone calls. She bought it all. She was eating out of the palm of his hand. Little did she know he was just a nice boy from a tight family and the farthest possible thing from a gangster. None of the reality mattered, though—it was all about what she perceived. It was all about her perception of him, and he mastered the art of putting on a good show. He knew that by putting on the gangster thug act, the likelihood of her liking him was much higher. He was right on the money. It was what she *perceived* that mattered. She valued the dangerous thugged-out type, and he added much value to himself in her eyes by playing that role.

It wasn't about keeping the girl in the long term. It was about making her believe what he believed she would value. I am not espousing that we should be fake or phony, but at times many people want to be perceived in a certain way in order to get what they want. It's about adding value to something, whether to yourself or to something you're selling. It is all about added value for the benefit of the actor, especially if he knows what the other person values, so he can tailor his behavior (and appearance) accordingly.

Added value makes things more appealing and makes people want to have them more. Since we are governed purely by self-interest, the more value something has, or we perceive it has, the more we will want it. There are millions of people in North America who get paid ridiculous amounts of money for trying to add increased value in the minds of the public by manipulating how people perceive things in order to sell products, get votes, or look better. They do just about everything to bend the truth a little to have people perceive the world in a way that is in the actor's (or company's) self-interest. This applies to anyone and anything, from a used car salesman selling a painted-over rust-bucket, to a huge ad campaign pumping up the new extreme sports drink or politician. At times, the substance of what something is matters much less than the value-laden fantasies we attach to it.

88

Remember this golden rule: it's what people perceive something to be that is important, more than what something actually is. Perception is everything. If I convince my friend that I have a baseball that was a home run ball hit by Babe Ruth, his perception of that ball's value will increase if he believes what I am telling him. But if I am just telling a lie, then the truth of the matter is that it is just a baseball. Perception is at the heart of human behavior. It builds our value systems by managing a lifetime of environmental inputs. It is at the heart of the thoughts that run through our heads. Misperception is also at the heart of numerous phobias, anxieties, eating disorders, compulsions, odd behaviors, superstitions, psychopathologies, and countless other behaviors.

Perception and behavior is also affected by our sex. Women and men are from different planets mainly because of biology, which makes us think differently. Your sex is determined by the genes that your father has mixed with your mother's. It is the material in the male's sperm that will determine your sex. Females can only supply the X chromosomes, but males have either an X or a Y that commingles with the X in the embryo to determine a child's sex. If someone is XX they are female, while XY is male. The mere fact of having an X or Y chromosome next to the X we get from our mother makes us think differently right off the bat, all else being equal. Men are predisposed to perceive things differently from women simply because of genetics, which inevitably affects how we behave. For example, females innately want to nest and males innately want to spread their seed.

One such example of a predisposition to high value behaviors are those evident because of the maternal instinct. An example of this is the mother protecting her young, sometimes to their own demise, in almost every species on the planet. This specific "maternal instinct" is exclusive to and only possessed by the female/mother as the term implies. The capacity of the female maternal instinct far supersedes that of her male counterparts. This in turn affects how the sexes behave in response to the actions of, and threats to, their offspring. Every woman has the ferocity of a female lion when it comes to their maternal instinct and their offspring. This instinct is especially dangerous when it is converted to scorn. It is this invaluable instinct that promotes the survival and flourishing of a species. This instinct is a necessary part of the female arsenal in that it promotes the continuation of the family tree and survival of its genes into the next generation.

Another example of chromosome specific predispositions highlighting male/female differences is in the realm of pain tolerance. Women generally have better and longer pain tolerance than men. This is specifically tied to having an XX as opposed to a XY for one's sex chromosomes. This again will affect behavior in response to pain stimuli simply because of XX as opposed to XY.

Women also have better peripheral vision than men on average. So when you're gazing at that girl of your dreams and you don't think she can see you, think again. Not only do women have these idiosyncratic traits because of their XX, they also have the "Mercedes" model of the human body compared to that of their male counterparts. Never underestimate the resilience and nurturing capacity of the female body.

Men were not shortchanged in this exchange, as they possess the Y chromosome, which generally makes men physically stronger and less emotional than women. There are many subtle differences between males and females in the perception of the real world via their senses simply because of being XX or XY. With this in mind, we have to find a way to have harmony with one another and find ways for these specific traits to complement rather than clash with one another. This isn't always easy, as most of you know. Men are mechanical robots with simple pleasures, and women are delicate flowers with radiant petals and specific needs. Nevertheless, we must always coexist and mate to push humanity and knowledge along its intended path. This necessitates men and women relating to one another amidst a myriad of differing predisposed chromosome-specific behaviors.

I have always wanted to help people. Many people have taken my advice and I have made many more feel at ease within a few minutes of talking with them, especially when I have firsthand historical context of their situations. If I don't have the contextual background, the process of diagnosing the problem is a little more laborious. I must get some contextual history from the "patient" in the situation at hand so I can attempt to "fix" the problem. When I deal with people, I try to see through their eyes. I always try to put myself in people's shoes. It helps me make them feel better, and I can cater to their self-interest better if I try to see what they see and bring them value in line with their interests.

People will like you more if you cater to their self-interests by knowing what they like and being accommodating to them as much as possible. It takes practice, but we must make attempts to see ourselves operating in the world through the eyes of others around us. It is the little things that can make a big difference when dealing with others. People can get very annoyed if you treat every situation as though it's all about you, even though it really is.

I like to talk about myself. I begin a lot of sentences with "I". I have to make a conscious effort not to begin sentences with "I". When someone tells me something like "I went to Las Vegas," my first instinct (and probably a lot of other people's) is to reply by saying "I _____." For example, when my friends came back from Las Vegas, they would say something about the Bellagio, and I would say, "I ate at the buffet there and it was to die for" or "I love the fountains there" or "my friend and I went shopping there." This is annoying to others.

Remember it's all about me (you), but don't make it all about me at the expense of others because people don't like that. People want their stories to have the value that they perceive them to have, even though nobody really gives a shit about the amazing lunch that I had at the Bellagio buffet in Las Vegas. If anything, it is a negative thing for people to hear unless they truly cared that I was rested, well-fed and felt good, something a parent would value but an acquaintance might not.

Being a good friend is about listening, giving, and letting people have a chance to bask in the glory for a few seconds about what they did or where they went, even if your smile and nod are a bit robotic. Social interaction lies at the core of what we value. People value good friends who give, listen, and care. After all, social interaction is one of our basic human needs. We all seek it out in one form or another. Besides, what good is a good story if you have no audience to tell the story to?

In conversation, I now make a conscious effort not to begin sentences with the words "I" or "My". It is hard to do because we perceive and respond to everything through ourselves first, but there is nothing worse than people who continuously talk about themselves. It is better to be perceived as an underdog sometimes. We have to have balance, not too much of anything. It is hard to see yourself or notice that you talk about yourself so much. But it's nothing to be ashamed of. Just be cognizant of those around you and what you say and do because people are listening and watching. Think about what you are going to say and the implications of what you utter. Will it be offensive? Should I say something at all? Will I hurt someone's feelings?

Remember that it is all about you. It is all about the actor and bringing value to his vessel. You are the actor in this world, and all you do is seek out value for your vessel every second you are awake. You must tread lightly though on how you go about achieving that value. When someone tells you something, you think, *how does that affect me?* However, you might respond by saying, "I've seen that big hotel in Vegas, too" or "I saw that movie" or "I have been to that restaurant too." See what I mean? I began all of those responses with "I" and that usually puts a damper on the story my friend is telling.

Now I respond by saying things like, "Oh, that hotel must have been so nice," or "The food at that restaurant must have been awesome." This gives the speaker more investment in what they are telling you. It is fodder for their story; even though you could really care less that they had jumbo shrimp at the hotel, they will like you more if you just listen to them.

As much as we love to talk about ourselves, which is actually healthy, we must achieve that balance of not being overly self-centered and tuning in to what others are telling us. By bolstering people's stories and allowing them to communicate freely, they will like you more in the long run because you are the rapt audience that gives value to their story and makes it worth the experience. That is what being a good friend is about. People value others who can listen and admire them a little bit—even only for a few seconds. It is their perception that you care and that you are truly interested in what they are telling you. Of course, as anyone who has been backed into a corner at a cocktail party can tell, it gets a little out of hand when you reinforce people with too many "you must haves" and they can't find a way to shut the hell up. That is why balance is the key. Give to your friends. Give them what they value, but keep it balanced. If you don't, they will start to trample too heavily on your own interests.

Perception is at the heart of the reason why we behave in the ways we do. We assign value to things in the environment based on the qualities we perceive them to have. It is this value we attribute to certain things that pushes us in different directions. Everyone on earth is in pursuit of reinforcement, be it positive or negative. We are all hedonists. We all seek pleasure and want to avoid pain. Nobody likes pain of any kind, be it physical or emotional. Those few that do like pain like it because it feels good to them. For example, someone who is a masochist actually likes having painful things done to them because they enjoy it. It is reinforcing to them. They will behave in ways that will lead to pain being inflicted upon them, not because it is punishment as a scientist would term it, but as an enjoyable positive reinforcement. I give this example because I know there are those who, when reading those few sentences above about everyone being a hedonist will say, "No, I like pain! I like to be punished."

Punishment, in its purely scientific sense, is a stimulus that is inflicted upon a subject; it is a stimulus that the subject truly dislikes or deems as having negative value, such as a hard slap to the face. This is thought to diminish the likelihood of the subject repeating whatever behavior he or she was punished for, with the caveat that the subject makes the connection between the punishment and the undesired behavior.

I have seen a mother slap a young child's hand for spilling soda on the floor minutes after it happened. The mother thought that by slapping the child's hand minutes apart from the undesired behavior she wanted to discourage (spilling the soda), the child would stop spilling. She failed to appreciate that the child would unlikely make the spilling-punishment connection because of the distance in time between the occurrence of spilling and punishment. I knew with almost 100 % certainty that that child would go back for that soda and do it again. What the mother assumed was punishing to the child was not, insofar as spilling was concerned. The mother became frustrated because she was puzzled as to why her strategy wasn't working. I saw into the future again by tapping into what each party (the child and mother) perceived. I could predict what each would do next because of the historical context and by knowing what each person perceived the situation to be.

I remember being punished by my mother when I was a young boy for swearing at my grandmother. In contrast to the last story, the punishment came close in time to the wrongful act. There was contiguity between the act and the punishment. Right after swearing at my grandmother, unbeknownst to me, my mother dabbed some red pepper on her index finger and without warning stuck her finger in my mouth and said, "Never talk to your grandmother like that again." That was punishment. It was a trick from the old country. It was swift and it was powerful. I was given a salient negative stimulus quickly in the hope that I would refrain from exercising my new vocabulary. It worked wonders. I never swore at my grandmother ever again.

Countless studies have demonstrated that punishment works best—to decrease the likelihood of the behavior occurring again—when it is swift and salient, right after the event or undesired behavior has occurred. I agree with the opinions of countless psychologists who feel punishment should only be used as a last resort to curtail highly undesired harmful behaviors in severely mentally challenged people. Punishment has been used for decades in certain institutional settings where the mentally challenged are cared for and all else has failed. Examples of punishment include electric shocks, slapping, spanking, and really anything punishing. Some of these mentally challenged people purposely strike their foreheads into corners of walls, cut themselves, and do other harmful things causing severe damage to their bodies. Due to their compromised cognitive repertoire, traditional behavioral modification techniques failed to stop many of these acts. As a last resort, each time a child would begin the self-inflicting harm they would be shocked, spanked, yelled at, and have other negative events presented to them. These punishers, singularly, or in combination, came immediately after the harmful undesired behaviors. The punishment was swift and uncomfortable. In many instances, the self-mutilating behavior ceased altogether. Thus, punishment should only be used as a last resort when the benefits outweigh the costs, such as in the treatment of mentally challenged self-mutilators.

If punishment is a last resort, the keys to its usefulness are swiftness and strength, close in time after the undesired behavior. This is why people continue to get photo radar tickets for speeding. The deterring effect of the fine is weak because punishment comes so far after the undesired behavior (speeding) that is neither swift nor salient. However, it is a cash cow for the municipality. For those who think photo radar makes people drive slower, keep lying to yourselves and the public. It has very weak punishing effects.

The other type of behavioral model that seeks to prevent certain behaviors from recurring is something called response cost. This involves taking away a positive stimulus from the subject so they will not commit the undesirable behavior again. A classic example of this is loss of freedom enacted by being sent to your room or to jail. The loss of something *positive* (something we value) is the *cost* of our response. Like punishment, this works best when something is taken away quickly and has value to the actor after the undesired behavior is committed. So, when you take away your kid's keys to the car, do it right when they come home late as opposed to in the morning.

Each of us strives to achieve positive and negative reinforcement every second that we are awake. We try to avoid punishment and avoid acting in certain ways that cost us things that we enjoy, such as our freedom, as long as we feel the costs outweigh the benefits. Sometimes this pursuit of pleasure and avoidance of pain are at odds with one another. A junkie who wants a hit of crack will go out and buy some because the reinforcing effects of the drug are so powerful, even though the purchase may land him in jail and cost a fortune in the long run. When the chances of being caught are minimal, and the effect of the drug is powerful enough, the perceived costs are outweighed by the perceived benefits. The junkie buys it up, gets high, and on he goes.

Perception is the nucleus of human behavior. Without our sensitive sense organs constantly processing these inputs from our environments, life would be extremely mundane and predictable. Our idiosyncratic view of the world via our senses is the spice of life, so pay close attention to what is going on around you. Don't be fooled or taken for granted by your significant other. Stand up and be strong. One-sided relationships are for the weak and vulnerable. Be cognizant of what elements in the environment are causing you to act in a certain way. Analyze and process inputs into your senses. Was it something you heard or something you saw? What does it mean to you? Stop and reflect on the situation and take it all in. Think before you speak or act. Then make your next move.

CHAPTER 8 - The Secret of *The Secret*

I was sitting with a client on a patio downtown on a hot June day. We were chatting casually when he brought up a book called *The Secret.*[1] He asked me if I had heard of it. I replied, "Yeah, I watched a bit of the DVD."[2] He said, "I follow the principles in the book, and my girlfriend is doing it, too." He insisted that it worked. It is a book that is supposed to change your life and the way you live. He was absolutely convinced that this book had made a significant difference in his life. I was a little skeptical and cynical, as I am with many things. I didn't really put much more thought into the book and wrote it off as black magic or delusion.

A couple of months later, I flew to Los Angeles and stayed with a longtime friend in West Hollywood. He had the same book on his shelf. One night, when he and his girlfriend went to sleep early, I thought I would give this book a read. As I read the book, I became even more skeptical towards it. The book states that the universe follows the laws of attraction, and if we manifest thoughts of what we are attracted to and what we want in life, those visualizations and manifestations will come to fruition. Essentially, think *it*, and *it* will come. Think positively and positivity will come. Think negatively and negativity will come. Feeling blue? Do something fun.

If positive thinking has any efficacy in relation to this book, it's in that it deals with attraction, which goes hand in hand with self-interest. Attraction is just a synonym for interest. We are attracted to things that we have an interest in getting, and we are interested in things that we are attracted to. We are attracted to things that matter and things that matter have value to us. If it serves our wants and needs, we will be attracted to it: the laws of human behavior are firmly entrenched. It is by the universal laws of human behavior, comprised of our genetic vessels crashing through the environment in the pursuit of self-interest via logical lawful behavioral principles that our lives unfold as they do. The environment and one's idiosyncratic genetic makeup determines the value and attractiveness of things.

The Secret's message of positive thought is a good one and a good starting point. We all have hopes and dreams and we all feel the pull of "Wouldn't it be nice to..." as we envision our wants as fantasies that we hope will come true. We get what we want in life by what we say and do. We act and speak in our pursuit of our self-interest. Genes play a massive role in this process, as does the environment. You can think as hard and as positively as you want about something, but there are no strong positive correlations between positive thoughts and positive outcomes. It's an illusion for all of those people out there who invest too much into the slight benefits of positive thought and think that certain outcomes in their life are inextricably tied to the fact that they were thinking positively about a particular thing they desired. There is no cause and effect at play here. There are only loose correlations at best, which doesn't mean much in the real world.

A reader of *The Secret* may encounter a positive experience and attribute it to the book. Thinking positively may move you in the right direction and make you feel a little better, but there is way, way, way more to the equation than just "think good, and good will come." Those who overemphasize the value of positive thought because of a certain outcome they encounter are just blind to what is called temporal or spatial contiguity and coincidence.

The Greek philosopher Aristotle wrote about the laws of association and contiguity. Contiguity can be either spatial (in space) or temporal (in time), or both. Association by contiguity means that things that are experienced closely in time and/or space tend to become connected or associated with one another in the actor's mind. This concept is well known and lies at the heart of classical conditioning.

The Secret serves as a beacon to those people who may have had a positive thing come to them after positive thought about it. The convinced actor, because of mere coincidence and contiguity, will continue to perform those similar behaviors in order to gain the value that they seek and have mistakenly attributed to the book and positive thought. This is the case even if those fortunes would have most likely occurred regardless of positive thinking. Many of the reviews I have read try to experiment with the principles in *The Secret* with little success. Positive thought has done little for me either. Again, positive thought isn't a bad thing but it is hardly anything in the grand scheme of our lives, and it takes us nowhere if we don't speak and act in order to get what we desire.

The laws and principles you read about in this book are the true secret of the inner workings of human behavior. Understanding and educating yourself is the single most important factor in bringing benefit and value to your life and avoiding costs. Only cognizant understanding of why you do what you do can assist you in achieving your goals and get you where you want to be. What do you want? What do others that you interact with want? What are you going to say and do to get where you want to be? Are you behaving in a self-defeating manner? Are you attracted to dangerous and limiting things in your environment? Stop and take stock. Reflect. Understand yourself. Make a contract with yourself to change your ways if you need to via knowledge and education. You will be so happy when you crush those obstacles in your way. Do it for yourself. Again, educating yourself on why you do what you do is the biggest step in the direction for self benefit.

The law of purpose and value-driven human behavior is the law of the land. We are all hedonists seeking out pleasure and avoiding pain. Thinking positively is just a foot in the door. It puts what we value into perspective and allows us to focus more clearly on it. Thinking positively affects our perception of the things we value in the environment. It allows us to add value to the importance of attaining those things we desire and makes it only slightly more likely that those things will come to fruition in the real world.

Positive thought is a method of honing our affinity for what we desire, but getting to the end point involves plenty more than just positive thought. It is a good head start to remaining focused on the prize. However, you may or may not get it depending on your resources and what you say and do. After all, we are simply actors among a myriad of other actors wanting many of the same things. Unfortunately, if we don't have the ability to attain the resources to make something we want happen, then it cannot be achieved. If we don't understand the mechanisms and elements driving our actions, we will stumble many times on the way to achieving our goals—if we ever even get there.

We also have different capacities for different things depending mainly on genes and less on environment. Capacities matter. You need the genetic capacity right out of the gate, or it's a frivolous endeavor. That isn't to say we don't make valiant attempts to get where we want to be. We put ourselves to the test and push our limits. I remember doing arithmetic and geometric equations in math and my mental capacity began to sputter as I was at the end of my mental mathematical capacity. Certain people are just simply better than others at certain things, and will attain different things purely because of genetics. It is our genes that give us our starting vehicles for the game of life. Some people can never become professional hockey players or professional football players no matter how hard they try. They just don't have the genetic capacity. Some will never become mathematicians—again they just don't have the capacity. Positive thought is a method of honing our affinity for what we desire. Getting to the end point involves plenty more than just positive thought. If you lack the capacity and, to make matters worse, you live in a poor learning and training environment, you will never reach that destination, no matter how hard you think or try.

It seems the more positively I think about things, the worse the outcome is. That also flies in the face of *The Secret's* doctrine. Your predisposed genetic faculties predetermine the depth of your physical and mental capacities, which can then be fine-tuned by the environment and training. So, contrary to what your parents told you, you can't be or do whatever you want. I don't mean to discourage you because you can still be a lot of things. We all must strive to reach our dreams and goals, even if we fail. If we don't try, we will never know.

I was having an argument with a friend of mine after he said "anyone can be anything they want to be." I bluntly responded "that's not true." He maintained his statement and I maintained mine. Unfortunately, we all have genetic and environmental limits on what we can become and who we can be. As mentioned, certain people can never become a medical doctor, a hockey player, a football player, or a mathematician, no matter how hard they try, even if given all of the environmental resources needed for the task. If someone lacks the foundational requisite genetic "soup" for a certain capacity, then he or she can never become anything they want to be. Think positive all you like. Genetics are the single most important variable in human behavior and success.

Barack Obama, an unlikely candidate for president, won the presidency because he had all of the genetic "tools" along with a fertile environment in which to thrive. It was unbelievable and unthinkable that an

African-American could accomplish such a feat at such a young age at that point in American history. In order to have done so, he needed advantageous genetics for the task which are evidenced by his vast intellect, reasoning, and oratory skills, even evidenced by his actions in college. It also helped to be in a political environment hungry for a change of the status quo. His genetic soup was at the right place at the right time and he delivered with flying colors, because it was the lawful result of the interplay of his genetics and environment (context).

Unfortunately, all those people out there who have subscribed to this overemphasis on positive thought will inevitably discover there will almost always be a disproportionate amount of return to the downside, in comparison to the positive outcomes desired by the actor. *The Secret* is a smart book for taking advantage of the law of contiguity, and it does a great job of marketing the book as a mystical hidden treasure open only to the chosen few who will commit to living by its principles. Reading the book, and having one of your positive thoughts come to fruition may lead you to quickly associate your new life treasures with the reading and use of the principles of *The Secret*. After this you will go on to tell your friends until everyone is sucked into this erroneous vacuum of hope. Don't fall into that trap—it's nothing more than coincidence and contiguity. What's even worse is that the book may be turning people away from proper intervention in their lives because they are hung up on the erroneous proposition that their continued devotion to positive thought will make things better. Get up and take charge. Talk and do more if you want something good to happen to you. Thinking positively is good, but nobody will be ringing your doorbell anytime soon holding a basket of your wishes. Nonetheless, I always try to remain a positive thinker who tries to see the good in things. I also strive to do well and feel good. Positive thought won't hurt, but it is only a starting point. The interesting part of the story is when we turn our thoughts into words and actions. Ultimately, success has to do with what we say and do with our genetic vessels in the environment we are in. Educate yourself and understand the building blocks of your actions. It is then that you can alter your behavior by achieving what you want and avoiding danger or pain.

CHAPTER 9 - The Continuum of Human Behavior

Human behavior can be thought of as being on a continuum. On one side are involuntary reflexes, instincts, conditioned reflexes, stereotypical automatic archetypal responses and equilibrium processes. On the other side are thought-out, voluntary, conscious behaviors.

Involuntary reflexes are a small piece of the behavioral pie at one pole of the behavioral continuum. They are not governed by preconceived notions or conscious thought in order for them to occur. Reflexes are behaviors that are not voluntary—that is, we don't intend them to happen, hence the name. Reflexes make up a small fraction of the totality of human behavior. They are nevertheless noteworthy of mention because to omit this slice out of our behavioral repertoire would be like leaving the Mona Lisa without a smile.

In the realm of human behavior, involuntary reflexes comprise a piece of the behavioral mosaic that is hardwired into us just by the mere fact that we are *Homo sapiens*. For example, when you go to the doctor for a check-up, and he hits your knee with a mallet to test your reflexes, and your knee jerks up wildly, this is called the "knee-jerk reflex." Generally, we all have this reflex. This reflex occurs without conscious thought. It is built into our systems. Another example is the suckling reflex of a baby. When a mother's nipple, or something that physically resembles a nipple, touches a baby's mouth, the baby has an automatic suckling reflex that is immediately "turned on" by the stimulus to the mouth. When a small child gyrates to the sound of music, the response is natural and reflexive in nature. This innate sense of rhythm could explain why so many of us love music of one type or another and like to dance, and why music forms such a key part of human cultures everywhere. We all have these sets of reflexes: they are built into us, and they are with us at the time of birth.

Since reflexes are not considered voluntary actions, we cannot be held accountable for the consequences of these actions—because we never had control over them in the first place. My criminal law professor once defended a man charged with assault with a weapon. The accused was talking on a rotary telephone when another guy came up behind him, undetected, and severely startled him. In response, both of the accused man's arms jerked upwards, and he inadvertently hit the complainant in the face with the receiver of the telephone and was subsequently charged. His defense was that his behavior was involuntary, and because of this he was not in conscious mental control of his actions. He therefore committed the acts unintentionally, and could not be held accountable for them.

This was a crafty defense, because in criminal law the prosecution needed to prove what is called the *actus reus* and the *mens rea* of an offence — the guilty act and the guilty mind, respectively. For example, if you intentionally shoot someone, then the guilty act would be aiming the gun and pulling the trigger. From this deliberation, it would be inferred that you intended the behavior, so the mind is guilty as well. The prosecution's case would fail in the telephone example if it could not overcome the defense's argument of involuntary reflex because the accused lacked the guilty mind. That is, he never intended for that outcome to occur. He had no guilty mind, even though the act in itself was committed and could be labeled guilty. A person cannot be said to be guilty of a crime unless his mind is guilty as the offence is committed, and that person understood the gravity of the act. The defense in this case worked. The trial judge agreed that there was no *mens rea* (guilty mind), and therefore the accused could not be guilty of an act he didn't consciously intend to commit. The concept of involuntary reflexes is a small but crucial part of the realm of human behavior and something to keep in mind, for it is just another important piece of our behavioral mosaic.

Closely related to involuntary reflexes on the behavioral continuum are what are known as conditioned reflexes or responses. These occur because of association with stimuli in our environment. When people speak of Pavlov's dog, they are really speaking of a conditioned reflex/response. Ivan Pavlov (1849—1936) was a scientist, psychologist, and physician who unearthed a phenomenon known as classical conditioning. Because of his involvement, some name the concept "Pavlovian conditioning" in his honor. Pavlov worked to manipulate the behavior of animals by closely tracking their natural responses and subtly connecting these to a trigger (stimulus) that he controlled.[1]

In his best-known experiment, Pavlov used a bell as a stimulus to elicit reflexive salivating behavior in dogs. Dogs, of course, salivate in the presence of food when they are hungry, much like we do when we walk into a restaurant when we are starving. This is the automatically and naturally occurring unconditioned response. It is *unconditioned* because it occurs naturally from our hardwired processes. Just before placing food in a hungry dog's mouth, Pavlov rang a bell. After numerous repetitions, he found that the food and the bell had become so associated in the mind of the dog that he could make the dog salivate simply by ringing the bell—before the food was anywhere near. The dog became *conditioned* to salivate to the sound of the bell because of its previous associations with food. So the dog's *unconditioned* response to food, which was to salivate, had become associated with the sound of the bell, creating a *conditioned* response to the bell.

However, the animal must be *conditioned* in order for the natural response (salivation) to be emitted in response to a stimulus such as a bell. So now the salivation to the bell is a *conditioned* response, and the bell is the *conditioned* stimulus that elicits the *conditioned* response. Even when the bell was rung with no food in the area, the dog would salivate as if there were food in its mouth. This anticipatory behavior—salivation at the sound of a bell—takes advantage of our naturally occurring responses to things such as food. This happens because of past temporal and spatial contiguity of the bell and food in the dog's mind. Because of their proximity in space and time, they became associated with one another so that the sound of the bell elicits salivation due to its previous pairings with food. If we were to use a slightly different sounding bell than the bell that we conditioned the dog with, the dog would salivate, but slightly less. This is what is called *stimulus generalization* which I will discuss shortly.

Does a certain song or smell remind you of something so vividly that you feel those same feelings you felt when you first encountered that song or smell? Well that is because those associations are entrenched in our minds, and our reactions are conditioned responses to the naturally occurring feelings that were going on at the time. Things that are closely associated together in space and time may not elicit a reflex per se, but they might evoke thoughts or feelings of past associations when one of the stimuli is present. When you hear a song that is related to a specific event, and instantly think of those things that had contiguity with that song (a past girlfriend or boyfriend, your wedding day, a breakup, etc.), the associated feelings and thoughts you are emitting are conditioned responses.

What song takes you to that place of reminiscing? After a really stressful day at the office, I was driving home and listening over and over to a song by Eminem, Skylar Grey and Dr. Dre entitled, "I Need a Doctor." Just over two weeks later, on the weekend when I was feeling fine, I played the song again. Guess what happened? I began to feel that wrenching stress I felt that day at the office. I had unknowingly conditioned myself because of repeatedly pairing of anxiousness and worry with the song. So my conditioned response was to feel stress when the song was on, even though I really liked the song.

Smells also provoke these same emotion-evoking reactions based on past contiguity with certain stimuli. The smell of Fahrenheit by Christian Dior always elicits thoughts of the eighth grade in me. My thoughts are almost, if not certainly, reflexive in nature: they just happen. They happen because of a built-in system in our minds that associate things that are contiguous in space and time. This common thread runs through all human beings, no matter who they are. This is another lawful constant that makes us who we are and ties us all together with others and our environment via a common thread.

I was once in a bad car accident when I was proceeding through a green light and a car turned left in front of me. My car was written off. The girl who turned in front of me was driving her mother's beaten-up minivan and was only 15 years old at the time. Just before impact with the minivan, I slammed my foot on the brakes and skidded toward the van. I struck the van at an almost 90 degree angle and blacked out. I woke up with my car rammed into a light post and people surrounding the wreckage.

After this incident, I noticed that something changed in my behavioral repertoire. I find myself pumping my brake reflexively as I pass through a green light when someone is turning left in front of me. My behavior was conditioned from the accident. Let's break it down. The car turning left in front of me is analogous to the bell in the Pavlov example. That is the conditioned stimulus, because it causes me to react in a certain way just by its mere presence and past association with a previous behavior and feelings of fear.

The crash is analogous to the food, but instead of salivating it causes me extreme fear, which is a natural reaction to a crash. So, the car turning left has become the conditioned stimulus, and a lingering anxiety and fear are the conditioned responses—like the bell with no food. Hence, the sight of a car turning left (conditioned stimulus) in a situation similar to the accident causes me to pump the brake out of a conditioned fear to that situation. Just as the dog salivates to a bell, I brake pump to the sight of a car turning left as I proceed through a green light. It is an anticipatory response because of historical context and contiguity. The dog anticipates food from the sound of a bell and reflexively salivates. I anticipate an accident from the fear associated with a left-turning vehicle and pump my brakes.

You may have witnessed these anticipatory types of behaviors in your pets. These anticipatory type responses can be seen when someone grabs their dog's leash or shakes a bag of cat food. The pets will make associated responses to those items based on the natural responses invoked when encountered by the animal. My brake pumping behavior was conditioned to be reflexively acted out by an unpredictable, but associated-to-fear stimulus. We may find ourselves avoiding all types of situations or people because of their associations with fear in space and time. This avoidance is negatively reinforcing because it takes away something that we know we don't like (fear) and it makes that avoidance behavior more likely in the future.

Closely tied to conditioned responses or reflexes is what I call SAAR's (Stereotypical Automatic Archetypal Responses). The term came to me in one of my "eureka" moments in life. I was in the shower, staring at the tile on the wall in front of me with the water spraying on my back and neck. I was thinking about a question that my professor, Dr. Wardell, had asked the class in Psychology 271: *Personality* about 10 years earlier. The professor was talking about the emission of certain behaviors in our everyday environment. He told us how when he would get to his office he would, by "force of habit," use his house key to attempt to open the door to his office. He would get angry as the key he was trying to put in the lock wouldn't fit, until he pulled it up and realized it was the wrong key. He kept asking the class, "Why do I do that?"

With the water hitting my back in the shower, I was asking myself the same question. I was the student and the teacher at the same time, with a question that seemed to linger in the back of my mind over the 10 years. I asked myself, " **Why** would he do that?" *There must be an explanation. There has to be one because all behavior is lawful. It didn't just "happen." To the contrary, it followed laws. There is always an answer to why.* I asked myself again, "Why in the hell would he do that?" as I stood there in a deep moment of thought. I thought really hard with the water dripping down my face and staring at five shampoo bottles in a blank gaze. I found myself slipping into the fourth dimension of thought for a few seconds, and then all of a sudden. BOOM. It hit me like a sledgehammer. Sudden understanding crashed into me: I GOT IT! I KNEW THE ANSWER. I knew the *why*. It was due to a phenomenon called stimulus generalization. He was generalizing the stimulus of his office lock with his house lock and acting as if he was opening his house door.

I immediately turned the water off and dried myself quickly as I scribbled my ideas down on a parking ticket lying on my dresser. I hate to forget things I think about in the fourth dimension, because it is not an easy place to get to, and the thoughts there are like pearls in a seashell at the bottom of a deep sea. It was a happy moment for me. I couldn't wait to run down to the "laboratory" where my computer was so I could think this through. I had cracked the *why* once again.

When suddenly inspired, I always think of a story about Paul McCartney that I read in an article by John G. Sutton. He wrote,

> Paul McCartney of the Beatles tells the story of how he woke early one morning with music and the words of 'Yesterday' playing in his head. He immediately copied these down and one of the most frequently recorded songs of all time was born. Was that inspiration or perspiration? Now there is a saying that God helps those who help themselves and I sincerely believe this to be true. The initial phase is the real perspiration, the groundwork that goes in before inspiration can be interpreted with any meaning.[2]

Sutton presents McCartney as a master of his craft. He had the ability to receive and react to the inspiration he received through long years of development. He goes on to state,

> Our duty is to make ourselves available through preparing and mastering our God-given gifts. Be that as engineers, architects or creative artists. The idea that great writers, composers, poets and musicians sit down

and invent their work without inspiration is, to me at least unthinkable.[3]

I did my hard time of hours upon hours studying psychology in the library and going to hundreds of lectures. The inspiration was just around the corner, and I could not subsume it for too much longer. Thoughts continued to rear their heads in my mind and it was in their service that I began to write this book. It was inevitable. That answers the question of many who ask, "So what made you decide to just sit down and start writing a book?" Let's go back to my professor and his keys.

When my professor asked us why he tries to open his office with his house key, the answer is that he is committing a SAAR (Stereotypical Automatic Archetypal Response). This is the phrase I invented to describe the door scenario. Let's break it down. The professor walks up to his office door and attempts to open it with his house key. *Why?* Well, when he sees the door to his office he commits the stereotypical behaviors that anyone would commit when they encounter a locked door: grabbing their keys, picking a key from the bunch, and placing it in the lock. We seem to perform such routine behaviors such as opening a door with a key almost automatically, at times without actually looking at the key and making sure in our minds that it's the right key for the door. We don't stop and become ultra-conscious of what we are doing. We normally don't look at our keys and consciously think, 'this key opens this lock.' It is done more automatically than that, and numerous behaviors we commit occur in this fashion. If they didn't, we would be bogged down with our own slow, concentrated thoughts, which are not necessary for certain tasks.

When the professor encountered a door that needed a key, the door became an archetype demanding certain stereotypical behaviors in order to pass through it. He thinks '*door = key,*' but not '*which key to which door?*' He thinks this automatically without any concentrated conscious thought going on. We commit most of our behaviors in an autopilot-like mode based on what we have learned in the past. This includes behaviors like walking, talking, picking things up, opening doors, lighting a cigarette, eating, etc.

The stimulus of the house door is similar to that of the professor's office door. The stimuli become generalized in the actor's mind, and the professor commits the same stereotypical responses upon encountering a locked door. However, his stereotypical response, which is automatic, is committed due to the fact that the door is an archetype. It represents a certain cluster of stimuli that elicits these certain responses due to previous historical interaction with doors, or a stimulus that anticipates door opening. The situation (context) of opening the house door was so similar to the office door that the erroneous response was committed on its own. The same thing happens to all of us in a multitude of situations.

One of my editors committed a SAAR after a meeting we had one afternoon. I told him to meet me at my office just before noon, and that I was located on the sixth floor of the building. After our lunch meeting he came to my office with me. When we walked into the elevator he casually pushed the button for the fifth floor. But we needed to go to floor six. Why did he do that? He committed a SAAR. His condominium was on the fifth floor of his home building and he automatically went for the fifth floor button. He shook his head because he had just read this chapter. I asserted, "I'm glad you've experienced what I said about SAARs in real life." We had a chuckle. He shook my hand and left.

So much of how we behave is automatic due to the stimuli we encounter, based on historical context with those stimuli, or ones similar enough to our past experiences. SAARs may cause us to make mistakes sometimes, but if we were to concentrate deeply on every action we commit, life wouldn't be the same.

Closely tied to involuntary reflexes in the behavioral milieu is the concept of imitation. I have always said that the purest form of culture is a function of geographic proximity. The closer you are to someone, the more likely you will behave like them, speak like them and share similar habits. This is a big part of what makes up the environmental side of who we are.

There are two types of imitation: hardwired imitation and imitation for reinforcement. Language is closely linked to hardwired imitation in that we have an innate capacity for imitating language, right down to the facial expressions of those who have reared us and cared for us. This goes far beyond the conscious level. For example, when someone is telling a story that you are very interested in, and that person is making slow and concentrated sounds with his mouth, you will sometimes find yourself unconsciously making the same facial movements and facial expressions as you listen to the story. I call this the "Echo Effect."

When my four-year-old niece looks at me and repeats a statement that she hears her mother say, she makes almost exactly the same eye and mouth movements as her mother makes, with the same facial expressions. She doesn't make these gestures because she was previously reinforced for doing so. They are just copied unthinkingly by observing her mother's facial movements. That is why smiling induces smiles —it's just an echo. That is also why certain facial behaviors, such as yawning, are contagious. Our hardwired imitative propensities make us mirror the facial acts of those around us. That is why true culture is a function of geographic proximity.

Echoes are closely tied to involuntary reflexes but are more to the centre of the behavioral continuum than are true involuntary reflexes. They are closer to conscious behaviors because they require some form of attention to the stimulus that they are mirroring in the first place. Involuntary reflexes need no conscious thought at all: they occur whether we like it or not.

When I was about seven years old, my brothers and I all had to go to the dentist. Once I was in the chair, the dental assistant came to prep my mouth for a procedure. This woman was shoving her fingers down my throat, and since I have a sensitive gag reflex, I immediately gagged. She screamed in my face, "Stop that!" She continued prodding, and I gagged again. I was sweating bullets at her cries for me to stop because I knew I couldn't help it. I was traumatized as she yelled, "I said stop that!" What an idiot she was. It was an involuntary reflex that I had no control over. I couldn't consciously just decide that I was going to stop gagging. It was a sensitive reflex that was hardwired into my reflexive repertoire and not something in my control. How could a dental assistant not know that?

The other difference between involuntary reflexes and hardwired imitation is consciousness of emitting imitative behaviors. If, for example, we mimic facial expressions when someone is telling a story, we can make a conscious effort not to imitate them. On the other hand, if a reflex is set to occur, it will usually occur regardless of our efforts. Hardwired imitation is something akin to a reflex in that we all have the capacity as human beings to produce sounds and facial expressions like those of the people who reared us and taught us to speak.

On the other side of the imitation coin is imitation for reinforcement. When we witness an actor getting something that we perceive as valuable to us, we will tend to commit those same behaviors to assist us in the pursuit of our interests. Hence the phrase "Monkey see, monkey do." The monkey sees a successful action and then does the same. It does so because it is attracted to the value it believes it will receive by committing a similar behavior. We follow the lead of people all of the time in everyday life, in a multitude of situations. This is all part of our constant struggle for value.

Other behaviors we emit are directly related to what we perceive in our environment and what we anticipate or what we encounter. These mental processes have a direct effect on physiological bodily processes such as excretion, digestion, heart rate, etc. These effects occur because of the interplay of psychology and physiology. Disorders labeled as psychosomatic have to do with the ability of the mind to affect the body. "Psych" meaning mind, and "soma" meaning body, make up the term psychosomatic. Things that weigh on the mind, or events we anticipate occurring, can have profound effects on our bodies. The mind-body connection can lead to many aches and pains, stimulate vomiting, bowel movements, and elicit a whole host of other reactions.

As I write this, I can't help remembering how I would have an immediate need to go to the washroom minutes before I was to write any exam in law school, because of the effect of my mind on my body. Before a major exam, the buildup of stress would have me sitting on the toilet in one of the washrooms in the Law building. It was how my body reacted to intense stress. Some people vomit. Some people sweat. The mind-body connection is alive and well and can affect how we physically feel and operate.

The behavioral continuum has at one pole completely involuntary reflexes, instincts, equilibrium actions related to homeostasis, subconscious processes, and conditioned reflexes, etc. At the other pole, are completely attentive, thought-out behaviors. Echoes, psychosomatic behaviors and SAARs lie closer to the middle of the continuum of human behavior. The further away we are from involuntary reflexes along the continuum, the more conscious we are of our actions. Thus, echoes are slightly more conscious than reflexes and instincts, and SAARs are slightly more conscious than echoes. Highly attentive, thought-out, and concentrated behavior is at the far end of the continuum of human behavior. So pay attention to the things you do, and stop and think where that behavior you just committed falls on the behavioral continuum. Assess why you did what you did. Become more conscious of why you are behaving as you are and why you acted that way. Knowing this is paramount in the matrix of behavioral modification paradigms and the ways we come to understand our own actions.

CHAPTER 10 - Relativity and Reward

As human beings, we have the capacity and the ability to remember what has happened to us in the past. With these past events entrenched into our minds, we know what our human vessel values and what we need to do to get that value and avoid value loss. This is where historical context really matters. The culmination of our life experiences directs us to those stimuli that we idiosyncratically have found to bring us value.

Our genetic vessels clash with the environment and by trial and error we become attuned to those things that are rewarding to us and those that are not. Once we know the protocol of reward from past experience (getting a positive stimulus or removing a negative one), we continue to behave in certain ways in order to satisfy our hungry self-interest in ways that we know to work. We act in certain ways and commit certain specific responses, many stereotypical, that we remember brought us reward in the past. Because of past reward and the corresponding value brought to our vessel, we will more likely commit those same behaviors in the future at a greater frequency, because of the laws of reinforcement.

When it comes to reward, the human vessel has an affinity for remembering what needs to be done to achieve the reward outcome. If we didn't have this recognition and recall system, there is no way that the human race could survive, because our memories are at the heart of our existence and our continual quest for value.

Certain behavioral and psychological phenomena are always at play when we encounter our vast stimuli-filled environments littered with what we find rewarding. In the previous chapter, I spoke of stimulus generalization using the example of the wrong key being used to attempt to open a door. The flip side or inverse of stimulus generalization is stimulus discrimination. Stimulus discrimination is our innate ability to see two things as being *different*. We differentiate between the two things or situations and see them as different even if they share similarities, whereas when we generalize stimuli we see them as being the same or similar. These two concepts are at the heart of our behaviors in everyday life no matter what we are doing or where we are.

We all have a relativity compass when it comes to reward. We have an innate ability to contrast current reward with that of previous similar reward or lack thereof in certain situations and weigh their relative values. It is crucial to remember that value is weighed idiosyncratically by the actor, because value to one may not mean value to another. Every idiosyncratic vessel has within it an idiosyncratic scale that gives particular weight to the stimuli we encounter. These weights have differing values for everyone, even identical twins operating in the real world. Food is a great illustration of this concept. Two people from different walks of life eating the exact same foods will have differing and idiosyncratic opinions of them and give them differing values. This is based on what they have eaten historically and, again, genetics.

When we encounter a particular stimulus or situation we attempt to reference it into what we know about the situation from our historical context. When we encounter a person that looks just like a person we have encountered in the past, we both generalize and discriminate. Our minds do some mental gymnastics due to our previous memories of the person we knew before and a mental reconciliation process occurs. Our brain can remember and recognize things we have seen in the past and is able to rate them relative to what we currently see. These processes are at the heart of value capture. We will generalize because of the similarities between the two stimuli and discriminate because of the differences between them. They are seen as the same because certain similar characteristics cause us to make generalizations about the two stimuli.

We also make discriminatory observations and calculations, due to the fact that even though the two stimuli appear to be similar, they are in fact different. Hence, by these mental processes we understand that the two stimuli, whether people or cars, are similar yet different. There is an inverse relationship between these two processes that are always working in conjunction with one another. The more we discriminate, the less we generalize, and vice versa. It is these systems of object-and-situation recognition by previous historical interactions that allow us to continue on our selfish course for value.

We are no different than our ancestors who were hunters and gatherers, except now we do our hunting and gathering within the confines of dense urban centers. This may seem like a more structured and orderly environment for what we deem valuable to chase, which is different for everyone, even identical twins. The inner workings of the mind weigh the relative similarities/differences and value between objects and situations, allowing us to commit the behaviors needed for reward.

As the degree of disparity between two objects increases, so too does the degree of discrimination, while at the same time the degree of generalization decreases. As the degree of disparity between two objects or situations decreases, the amount of discrimination decreases and generalization increases. When two objects appear to us as identical, discrimination is zero and generalization is 100%. The objects can be side by side or compared to something we have seen in the past. The more intimate we are with these certain stimuli, the more accurate our ability to discriminate between them will be, which I will illustrate.

People at the university I attended used to mistake my oldest brother for my second oldest brother. I thought that was very strange. I couldn't understand how people could mix them up. They resemble each other but they have different body frames, heights, eye colors, hair, facial shapes, etc. It made little sense to me. Knowing my brothers so well and for so long, I could easily discriminate their differences. My eldest brother is oval faced and five foot nine, stocky, green eyes, whereas my second eldest brother is square faced and six foot two, brown eyes.

What I failed to appreciate at the time was our relative points of reference, attained from differing degrees of historical context. My historical context with my brothers was very rich, allowing me to sharply discriminate between them, whereas this was not the case with people that were less familiar with them. Some people with weak historical context for my two brothers generalized them as the same person.

The same thing happened to me and my younger brother, who used to walk through the law library and have people he didn't know say hi to him, thinking he was me. They were generalizing, believing two brothers were one and the same. Due to their weak historical contexts, many people couldn't discriminate between the brother sets.

A similar situation just happened to me, which I'm sure many of you can relate to. I was walking to the bank and saw a girl from afar coming down the escalator toward me. As I needed a new prescription for my glasses, my vision was not 20/20. With my visual acuity off, I mistook her for my hairdresser because my mind made a generalization that it was her because I could not see the girl up close. I saw long brown hair, similar hair style, similar skin tone, similar body shape, etc. I waved to the girl, thinking she was my hairdresser. As she walked closer toward me and my vision of her was improved I realized that it was someone else.

I wasn't able to discriminate between the two people, because I was like the people who mistook my brothers for the same entity. My ability to discriminate was impaired not because of weak historical context but because of weak eyes. Nonetheless, the same principles apply. Their minds played the same trick on them that my poor vision did on me.

I could give countless examples of these phenomena at play because they are happening every second we are conscious of our surroundings, but I think you get the point. Eureka! To me, this answered how we perceive and differentiate things, which is a highly debated topic in psychology. I finally got it, thanks to my poor eyesight.

When it comes to reward, there is also another phenomenon at play that makes us act in certain ways because of our previous historical context with reward. This process is called behavioral contrast. Behavioral contrast is tied to historical context based on a previous reward or experience, contrasted to a reward in the present moment. I like to use the term "reward relativity," because the actor places a relative value on the new reward based on previous experience with a similar or same reward.

Domjan explains reinforcement as such:

> Numerous studies have shown that the effects of a particular amount and type of reinforcer depend on the quantity and quality of the reinforcers that the individual previously experienced. Speaking loosely, the research has shown that a good reward is treated as especially good after reinforcement with a poor reward, and a poor reward is treated as especially poor after reinforcement with a good reward.[1]

I will give some real life examples, so you can be more attuned to what this means for you.

Whyology

Let's say that you went to a restaurant, and you had a poor meal and poor service. A week later, you wanted to try the restaurant again, because it was close to your office, and the second visit there you had a great meal and great service. Well, you will see that experience as more rewarding and especially good because of the relativity with your past poor experience. You would have graded the second experience more rewarding than you would have had you gone to the restaurant once and had the one good experience. This is called positive behavioral contrast. We view things this way because of reward relativity and act accordingly, many times not even realizing the principles behind why we are acting.

The opposite effect applies as well. Had you gone to the restaurant the first time and had a great meal and went back a week later and had an awful experience, you would rate that experience worse than you would have in the absence of the prior good experience. The same principles apply to numerous situations in life.

The more we see something as rewarding, the more likely we will commit those behaviors that brought about that reinforcer. When reward relativity deems a reward to be high because of previous less rewarding quality and/or quantity of that reinforcer, we will be more likely to act with more vigor to get that reinforcer. Again, the opposite processes apply as well. When reward relativity deems a reward to be less rewarding because of previous positive experience, we will act with less vigor to attain that reinforcer.

A friend of mine used to frequent a nightclub downtown that was fairly busy on the weekends. He went to this place every so often with the intention of hanging out with friends and possibly meeting a girl. The first number of times he went to the nightclub, he had a decent time, but nothing that great. Then one night, he met the girl of his dreams, and they dated for several months. After several months went by, they split up and he was again in search of a nice girl like the previous one. Meeting that girl at that nightclub made the value of that nightclub higher than if he had just went there the first time and met her because of his past history at the venue.

That being said, where do you think his nightclub of choice was after the breakup? If you guessed the same place, you're following me. He went back to the "well," chasing what was so reinforcing for him. The value added to the place because of his previous dismal experiences there made

118

that place all the more valuable to him after meeting that special girl. It was more valuable because it was highly reinforcing relative to his prior history there. His frequency of going to that nightclub increased after the breakup at a rate that was higher than it was prior to meeting that girl. Bottom line, that nightclub was a highly valued venue to him.

Historical interactions with our environments will cause us to act in certain ways in the future. We generalize, discriminate, and make relative value measurements automatically, being the rough economists that we are, so that we act one way as opposed to another. These are just more of the universal laws of human behavior at play that we should all be in tune with if we want to understand what propels our behavior. The more knowledge we have about the processes that propel human behavior, the more we will be able to curtail or modify our behavior for ourselves and for mankind in beneficial ways.

By magnifying and highlighting the processes of human action, you will surely be better at understanding why you and others do what you do. Understanding these processes is essential to understanding our world at a deeper and more transparent level in order to bring about positive change in our lives. Changes we make have the best success under the umbrella of knowledge about what drives our behavior.

CHAPTER 11 - On Unexplained Variance

I can't help wandering through the psychology sections of bookstores; I think of it as collecting field notes in my everyday observation and experimentation. I was pulled into Judith Rich Harris's book *No Two Alike*.[1] Like a mystery novel, Harris delves into the unexplained and attempts to answer the following: *Why* is it that identical twins, reared in the same home environment, have differing personalities, opinions, and so on?[2] How can they vary to such a large degree? What factors are at work causing them to diverge from having the same personalities, biases and opinions? Since genes are held virtually at a constant in the behavioral equation, what was happening elsewhere to cause these differences or the variance in behavior? Harris seeks the answer to *unexplained variance* which has eluded psychologists for decades; those missing pieces of the behavioral and personality puzzle causing the differences in behavior and opinions among identical twins reared in the same households. Harris builds her argument with a wide range of studies and experimental results, so I picked up her book out of interest—but it only took me 11 pages of reading to start questioning her thoughts and forming my own answers.

The causal factors creating variance among twins are important because they are the keys to identifying which environmental stimuli shape and affect our behavior. This will assist you in identifying which environmental factors push and pull you in a multitude of directions and why.

Harris's book attempts to crack the code of unexplained variance. She uses the example of a pair of conjoined (stuck together) identical twins to show that these two people with almost identical genes and "identical" environments—as close as sharing a body—differed in personality and opinions.

Harris asserts, "...[I]dentical twins invariably differ in personality. Why they differ is a mystery that science has so far been unable to solve and that the twins themselves are puzzled by."[3] That is the beauty of this subject. We are all in pursuit of the same goal: the pursuit of the answers to the *why* of human behavior and human individuality. Harris points to the three systems of the mind—socialization, relationship, and especially status—as the answer to the mystery of unexplained variance. My answer to the puzzle or riddle of unexplained variance is called the *multiplicity of differential experience.*

Even though identical twins have nearly identical genes, they do not have identical environmental experiences—even if raised in the same households and even if they are conjoined. Moreover, there is no such thing as true identical twins. Twins that are termed identical because they come from the same egg and sperm are not exact copies of one another. Their subtle differences in genetics are part of the answer to unexplained variance. We can think of identical twins like cookie-cutter gingerbread men. They appear to be the same. However, if we measure the exact amounts of sugar, salt and flour in each of the gingerbread men, there will be differences. So too, will there be slight differences in the genetic codes of "identical" twins. Even identical twins start the game of life in slightly different genetic vehicles.

As each piece of environmental stimuli hits our senses, it is processed in similar ways, but we give particular meanings and value to things based on principles of reinforcement, discrimination, generalization and so on. Slightly differing experiences (even in the womb), with slightly different meanings will be built upon one another like a beautiful temple with its own unique intricacies and striations. These experiences will also have slightly different meanings for each of us, due to mechanisms such as relativity, which is based on previous experiences. Our value systems are built idiosyncratically on our exclusively unique genetic base, which forms the basis for individuality and personality. Our mind's supersensitive ability to process information from the external world is so specialized and unique that it allows behavior and personality to unravel and develop idiosyncratically, even with identical twins reared in the same environment.

What may be of similar importance is the effect of each twin on the other, which is undoubtedly a factor in their diverging personalities. Because twins are so similar, they act on each other's personality, shaping them and reinforcing them, inevitably making each person unique. Just as in physics, every behavioral action has an opposite and equal reaction. When twins are reared together, their individuality becomes clearer and more evident the older they become. Once these slight differences begin to crystallize, they proliferate, growing upon one another, in diverging directions from the other twin. As identical twins are not exact copies of one another genetically, they don't attribute value to environmental stimuli in the exact same way. This goes back to attributing value to our environment throughout our own unique set of genetic goggles. Minor variations present in the genetic codes of identical twins make them slightly different value chasers from the start.

Although twins are composed of virtually the same matter and genes, their value hierarchies have their own subtle and specific manifestations and idiosyncrasies. It serves a purpose to think differently than one's twin counterpart. It creates a sense of identity and individuality that is at the heart of self-interest theory. We each want a specific identity for ourselves so that we may increase and make it more likely that we can attain personal value. Twins may dress the same but they still value individual opinion, critical thought and self-determination. Of course, thinking of free will, individuality has an inherent value. Minor variations in genetics and environmental experience and the push-and-pull effects that the twins have on each other's behavior in the struggle for value create a slow metamorphosis toward individuality.

It is these subtle and minute differences and nuances of experience and genes that create the start of two slightly diverging paths as identical twins age, creating variance in the long run. These differences continue to morph and build on one another, creating the divergent personalities of identical twins. These subtle differences cause our behaviors and attitudes to proliferate over time to help us become truly unique people different from anyone else. The twins react and act toward each other in completely different ways, carving out their own individuality as they do so.

From the time in the womb until they develop, identical twins each experience differential developmental noise, differential experiences, differential subconscious leaks into the conscious and vice versa, differential random events, differential reinforcement, differential exposure to one another, differential nutrition, differential exposure to viruses and bacteria and so on. This multiplicity of experiential differences, coupled with slightly different genetic starting points, translates into differential personalities even among identical twins in the long run.

Moreover, twins make conscious choices to do things that set them apart from their siblings, as this adds to their struggle for identity and

122

individuality. There is no "me" without individuality, and it's all about me (or you). As these minute differences unravel and materialize in their own specific ways, the picture begins to get clearer as to the variance in the two "twin" entities. The possible number of behavioral outcomes, based on seeking value, build upon another until the number is almost infinite. Thus, it is clear why identical twins have differing personalities and so on. The possibilities are virtually limitless as to what each twin will value and be shaped by.

Once again, it all comes down to self interest, which is linked to individuality, which nears infinity on its own, because of differential experience and genetics. The multiplicity of differential experiences turns us into idiosyncratic value chasers, even if we have almost identical genes. This is the crux of individuality and the heartbeat of our unique personalities.

Differential environmental exposure—and attributed or assigned symbolic value given to those stimuli from that exposure based on genetics—builds value hierarchies that are as unique to each person as their fingerprints are. Reinforcement, be it positive or negative, along with genetics, is at the heart of these hierarchies. The behavior of identical twins, with identical genes—in a vacuum, free from any environmental exposure, with developmental noise held constant—would be identical. Thus, their geneavior would govern any movement or other actions absent any inputs to the senses. But that isn't possible in reality, only in theory.

It is the full exposure of ALL external matter, coupled with our genes, that allows our personalities to unravel in unpredictable, yet lawful, idiosyncratic directions. If roughly a billion self-interest behaviors are committed in the average lifespan, and then if we take a couple of identical twins that were reared together, each one of the twins would have committed roughly 12,500,000 behaviors after 15 years of life. As stated, these early self-interested behaviors are built on one another over 15 years, shaping our idiosyncratic behavioral hierarchies and value systems, due to the multiplicity of our differential experiences. They are like bouncing balls packed with our genetic "glue" bouncing in 12.5 million varying self-interested directions, acting in tandem with environmental inputs. The multiplicity of those bounces after millions of rebounds allows us to see the divergent paths of individuality and personality even among "identical twins". Whichever bounce you are clocking in at determines who and where you are at that moment in time. With that many self-interested bounces, it is no wonder that after many years of value-chasing identical twins have differing personalities.

The intricate details of human behavior and individuality chases infinity, as those millions of self-interested behaviors move us in slightly differing, yet potentially infinite directions. The near infinite possible amount of ways the behavior of mankind unravels due to layered differential experience built on our unique genetic vessels contains the answer to unexplained variance. It is difficult to quantify and explain, because the answer lies near infinity. It is all built upon the finite sequence of moment-to-moment actions that are linked to one another and tied to our supersensitive senses processing the environment and giving it unique symbolic value. These minute intricacies multiply on each other exponentially, snowballing to create unique people, even those with virtually identical genes.

CHAPTER 12 - Tell Me Lies

Why is it that some people lie all the time and others are painfully honest? People lie simply because the perceived benefits outweigh the perceived costs: the act of lying can be very reinforcing for some, giving them the propensity to lie in the future.

As you may know by now, lying is all about value. A man of integrity and honor will not lie because he values the truth and his reputation, for if he didn't, he wouldn't be a man of integrity and honor in the first place: social censure outweighs the possible material gains. But even integrity has a price—just look at all of the rogue lawyers and other professionals out there. A few people I know lie all the time, but I don't need to ask *why* they are lying. If I delve deep enough into them, I can figure it out.

Every lie is awful, yet lawful. Those who have been raised in environments where they are taught and rewarded to value honesty will likely see being honest as being more valuable than being dishonest. We all have lied in our lives. Why did we do it? Why did you lie to your wife or your girlfriend? *Why*? Think about it. You did because the benefits of lying outweighed the costs.

Being a lawyer, I know the art of lying quite well. No, it's not because I lie: believe it or not, I value people who are upfront and honest. Rather, I get lied to all the time, especially by my own clients. They lie to me so that I can spin their stories and they can reap the benefits. Some want me to lie for them, which I will never do. One guy wanted me to do a deal for him that was so absurd that I had to cease acting for him altogether because he would not take no for an answer. He had taken in his brother's identification and social insurance (security) card and used them to qualify for a mortgage as his own credit was a mess. He came into my office and closed my door. He sat down and said "I did something for this deal that wasn't right but just push it through." He explained how he pulled one over on the bank manager by using his brother's ID to qualify for the mortgage.

As a lawyer, when conducting the purchase of a property for which a client is getting a mortgage, I represent both the bank (the mortgagee) and the client (the mortgagor) at the same time. So, I owe both the bank and the client representation to the best of my ability. Now how would the bank feel—or how would you feel for that matter—knowing I let a rogue slip through the cracks to your possible detriment, simply by failing to do what I was hired to protect you from. You'd be pretty angry, as would the bank.

My client was putting an enormous amount of pressure on me to push the deal through. I was the last obstacle in the bank's line of defense, essentially verifying by signing a declaration that the person in front of me was indeed who he purported himself to be. There was huge gain for him to lie because house prices were skyrocketing at the time, and he was going to flip the property in days to make a huge profit. However, in order for him to do that he needed me to lie to the very client I was working to protect: the bank. My supposed benefit was to be seen in a favorable light by this guy, and also the $1000 I would make on the deal. However, my costs were many, and they certainly outweighed the benefits. I told him I wouldn't do the deal for him and explained to him the ramifications of doing such a deed. He was insulted and bitter towards me. It was me who was going to lose in the long run, not him, so I declined to act for him.

Aside from flat-out lies, there are what we call half-truths. Half-truths are just what the phrase says: they are half true or only part of the story. For example, my ex-girlfriend just hated when I played poker at my friend's house. So, when she would call and ask me what I was doing I would say, "Oh I'm just at my buddy's, hanging out." What I forgot to say was that I was also playing poker. Had she known that, I would have had a whole song and dance from her, and I wouldn't have heard the end of it. I edited the truth purely out of self-interest, with some negative reinforcement at work: performing an action (the half-truth) to avoid a negative stimulus (my girlfriend flipping out and giving me some unnecessary grief). The last thing I need with pocket aces staring me in the face is my girlfriend on the other line throwing off my game.

Half-truths are less costly to the actor than outright lies because we feel less guilt when we tell a half-truth as opposed to a lie, causing less dissonance within ourselves. Half-truths can still work to achieve our interests, but they are less blunt and weigh less on the conscience. Half-truths are easier to tell and are more defensible when questioned, thus their utility is high. However, when something causing us to deviate from the truth becomes more valuable in the actor's mind, we are more likely to tell an outright lie because the benefits of lying will usually outweigh the costs. When lying and half-truths got us what we wanted in the past, the chances of us doing it again increase because we were reinforced for doing it.

As stated, the reason we lie is purely because of positive or negative reinforcement and avoidance of costs. However, if it is too costly to lie, then we won't do it. Every actor has his or her own price list embedded in mind. It is that list that will determine when we lie and what we lie about, or tell half-truths about. Remember, we are all rough economists always weighing costs and benefits based on what we perceive as having value. This determines what we will do next.

When politicians or other high profile people lie, it is for a valuable purpose. So, I ask, why do they lie? Well, they have to as far as they are concerned. As they are the actor, they know the score. They know the pros and cons of lying as opposed to telling the truth. There is so much at stake, and it can be very costly for them *not* to lie. Thus, they choose the path they deem necessary in the circumstances. It is a well-calculated risk that might only bring them minimal cost if it backfires. The benefits of lying, in their eyes, outweigh the costs of telling the truth. It makes perfect sense to them. And every time an average person lies it makes perfect sense why they did it as well. It makes sense to the actor. Just like any other type of behavior, lying is lawful.

There was a class I enrolled in while at law school called Techniques in Negotiation. Our final was to write an essay, and the question that we all had to answer was the following: "If you could lie and get away with it, with no consequences, would you do it?" I remember sitting there thinking *How can I answer this question?* I started writing just what I am writing here. Before I go on, let me just say that my professor was very intrigued with my essay response. Our professor was telling us about the essays she read and she said she was especially taken by one of the essays handed in that attempted to deduce a mathematical formula to the answer. I began by saying that if one was to lie, one would have to put a value or cost on the act of lying and what it meant to them. If you take morality out of the equation (i.e. honesty, integrity, etc.), then I said of course I would lie if I was to gain something of value. It goes like this: I can perform an action that will only bring me gain and no loss (because the benefits would *always*

128

outweigh the costs), so, leaving morality aside, there is no reason to tell the truth. If there was no downside, then lying would be a viable option because there are NO negative consequences or costs. The only downside to the equation was if morality was involved, or if one's conscience entered into play. Then the price of one's moral fabric would enter the decision making equation. That being said, these costs might be outweighed by the perceived benefit that one would believe was coming.

Many people in very high positions have compromised their integrity for benefits they perceived to be huge. This has been happening on Wall Street for decades. When someone lies to you, and you later find out and can't understand why, there is more investigating to do. There's always a reason, and lying is just another behavior that can be explained by the pursuit of self-interest and reinforcement. When lying occurs, it is lawful and rational to the person who is doing it. It all makes perfect sense.

CHAPTER 13 - The Good and the Poor

I remember I was in first grade, and the bell went off for recess. Outside the class were hooks with our names above them. On these hooks were our winter jackets, and next to mine was the hook for a kid named Bradley. This boy was able to walk but he was physically impaired to a great degree. The other kids and I noticed Bradley having extreme difficulty putting on his jacket. A lot of them ran for the doors to head outside. As I sat there and I watched him struggle, more kids ran from the scene. I looked around thinking, "Who is going to help Bradley?" As fewer and fewer people remained in the hallway, I felt a heightening sense of duty to assist him.

I put his toque on for him and then his jacket. This was followed by his mitts, his snow pants and finally his boots. Due to his condition this was quite a laborious and slow task. By the time we were both ready to go outside and play the bell rang, signaling the end of recess.

As the students watched Bradley struggle with his coat, each person seemed to feel responsible to assist him. However, as the number of people diminished and I was in closest proximity to him, my sense of responsibility went up greatly. That was the first time I ever missed recess, but my teacher was proud of me.

This is a phenomenon in psychology called the "diffusion of responsibility effect," which was described by Darley and Latané (1968).[1] Basically, the more people who are present when someone is in need of assistance, the less likely it is that any one person will stop to help. When there are more people present who you feel may assist someone, it is less likely that the value of negative reinforcement (i.e. removing a negative stimulus by walking away from an uncomfortable situation) will be outweighed by the positive reinforcement of acting (the perceived value of assisting the person). Even Good Samaritans are not immune to the diffusion of responsibility effect in that one's propensity to be a Good Samaritan is decreased when there are more people around. You feel it less valuable to help because you may have less of a pull from your conscience, and so on.

Imagine that you were with two strangers as opposed to 10. Imagine that one of them became seriously injured or ill while all else was equal. You would be more likely to assist the person who was injured or fell ill as the number of people around you decreased. This is because there is less diffusion of responsibility: the smaller the crowd, the less easily you can hide behind it. On the side of negative stimuli, acting would counteract the feelings of guilt for walking away. Acting would also counteract the feelings of social censure that attach more easily when you can be identified in a small group.

Giving assistance also has positive reinforcement when you feel good about yourself for upholding a personal moral code. Now, imagine that someone was hurt or injured in a sports arena with hundreds of people passing by. Would you be less likely to come to that person's assistance? I think the answer is 'yes.' That's because although the positive reinforcement to assist in this situation is pretty much the same as the last, there is nevertheless very little, if any, negative reinforcement in this example. With more people around, your role on the scene is diminished, and you are less likely to be censured on an individual level.

A true Good Samaritan may assist in the arena, because for some people the positive and negative reinforcement of assisting someone in need almost always, if not always, supersedes the costs of walking away. They will therefore come to the aid of someone in need. This likelihood of assistance will usually be lessened as the number of people around goes up, even for Good Samaritans.

As stated, there is a correlation between the number of persons present when someone is in need and the propensity to assist. When the number of people increases in a situation where someone is in need, your likelihood of assisting goes down. That is one of the reasons a lot of people in highly populated places have a "don't give a shit about Tom, Dick, or Harry attitude."

Following Milgram's urban-overload hypothesis,[2] it is valuable to be apathetic in a city like New York because of the dense population and the societal stratification. It is reinforcing (negatively) not to be bothered among the vast stimulation on the streets. New York, like other large urban centers, is a breeding ground for apathy towards other members of society. This is not a slur against New Yorkers. It's just that it almost becomes necessary to insulate yourself. It can and would happen in any similar society. New Yorkers are no different than anyone else. However, their culture and environment are different, causing them to behave in the stereotypical and apathetic manner that they do because it has value to them. These feelings and subsequent actions are evoked due to positive and negative reinforcement. What transforms people's attitudes is a lawful behavioral response due to the environmental stressors of large population centers, coupled with transportation issues, time crunches, overexposure to panhandlers, crime, homelessness, poverty, noise pollution, etc. It is just a lawful scientific response on a societal level that is "contagious" due to the environment.

I felt this effect take shape in me as I was walking down Robson Street in Vancouver. It was a nice sunny day, and Robson Street was alive and well with people all around. There was a lot of street activity, as would be noticeable in any major city. I was constantly asked for spare change at a frequency that I was not used to in my home city.

There were panhandlers by the dozens asking me for change, some getting in my face about it. This continuous bombardment of requests, some polite, some impolite, some lies, some truths, and some words that I could not comprehend, was becoming a real nuisance. I enjoyed walking Robson, as it was my first peek into "Big City" life—or at least "Bigger City" life. As I walked for hours, I found myself becoming increasingly indifferent to the stimuli that were not of value to me, and I started ignoring some of the people asking me for change. It was uncharacteristic of me to behave in such a manner. I began to truly understand what I call the "Manhattan Effect." That is not to say that New Yorkers don't care about their fellow man: of course, they do. They are no different in substance than anyone else. It's just that in larger capitalistic populated centers where social stratification becomes more pronounced, people's empathy is eroded by the vast amounts of human and other stimuli in the environment.

I also don't want to sound coldhearted or naïve myself. My home city was booming in 2007, and the number of homeless people here doubled. I work in the heart of downtown, and the number of homeless people I have encountered asking for spare change has risen substantially. I had a profitable year, so I found myself flipping one-dollar coins to the odd guy or girl asking for spare change, even though it makes panhandling more pervasive pursuant to the laws of psychology. I just thought that what they chose to do with the money was their business. However, when I flip that guy or girl that dollar, that dollar is a reward in the variable schedule of reinforcement that I spoke about earlier. Remember, from chapter 6, panhandlers are on a variable schedule of reinforcement because they know that as long as they continue to act by asking people for spare change, they will be reinforced at a variable ratio, and this will strengthen their propensity to ask for change.

For example, a beggar gets money from the first person asked, and the third, and the fourth and fifth, and the 10th, and then the 16th, and so on. They know that as long as they keep asking people for spare change, they will be reinforced *variably*. This creates the "junkie effect" in these people because they become hooked on a variable schedule of reinforcement. It is no different than the gambler who puts money on a blackjack table, except instead of winning a hand, they "win" the change dropped into their hands on a variable schedule. Neither finds it easy to escape this behavioral cycle. These scenarios follow the same lawful principles of psychology as that fateful night when I was playing roulette.

It's heartbreaking when I walk down the street and I see a homeless person lying on the cold cement, sleeping or telling me they are hungry. Many of us couldn't imagine sleeping outside all night away from our cushy beds and warm houses. It is easy to take things for granted when you have it all so nice and cozy. However, the major problems I have with giving homeless people change are twofold: the money may be used to fuel a drug or alcohol addiction, and secondly it will make it more likely that their behavior will continue due to the variable schedule of reinforcement on which they are operating. These two factors make it less likely for the person to get out of the "business" of panhandling. Nonetheless, I used to take the chance that the person, even though I am reinforcing their behavior, will at least do something good with the money, like buy food and not drugs or alcohol. However, my behavior has since changed. Now I buy them what they want to eat. That's it.

I was having a coffee on the side of a street during my lunch break downtown when a homeless person walked up to the patio. The patio had four tables, each with four chairs around it. I used to sit there after I ate lunch and have a macchiato and a cigarette before I went back to work. As I was sipping my drink, this homeless person I often see around walked up to the table of four people next to me. I see this homeless man a lot, and he always has his signature line: "Can I have 25 cents, please?" The man was skin and bones. He had a neat haircut, but his jeans were soiled. I noticed that his belt was pulled to the last hole, and that his jeans were one missed meal away from hitting the floor. The people just ignored the man for the first second and then one woman said, "I think I have a small bun," as she pulled out a bite-sized, sun-hardened bun from a bag. She held it up, no better than table garbage. I saw the despair in his eyes as he turned and ignored the woman. He walked to another table in front of me and asked a guy for money and was turned away. He then turned to me and said his signature line: "Can I have 25 cents, please?" But this time he added "I'm hungry" at the end of his signature question. I'd never heard him say this before until that day. There was no way I was going to let this guy walk away hungry as the smell of soup and sandwiches wafted out from the coffee shop. I felt so bad because it is not common to hear homeless people state that they are hungry after they ask for money. How could I let this guy walk away? I couldn't. It would have gone against all I believe in and value.

He was dealt a disadvantageous genetic hand and most likely grew up in a poor environment that prevented him from thriving. I asked the man, "What do you want to eat?" He said, "I really want a sandwich and some soup, please!" I replied, "Go into the shop and tell the woman to make you a soup and sandwich combo and that I'm paying for it." He entered the door a few feet away, and I saw the girl working inside wave her hand at me. I walked in too, just in case they thought he was lying. He was known around the area, and he was rough and dirty, but so genuine at the same time. I walked into the shop and said, "Make this guy a soup and sandwich, and I'll pay for it when I bring my cup in." I went back out and resumed my tranquil afternoon with the sun touching my brow, a fine coffee, and the best part of the cigarette that was still lit. The woman at the table next to me looked over and said, "That was so nice of you to do that." I was like the Good Samaritan. There was some diffusion of responsibility, even though the man was in no immediate peril. Nonetheless, I couldn't let that man walk away hungry. The woman who said that to me probably felt a little guilty because she could have easily done what I did, but she neglected to do so.

Whyology

A couple of minutes later, the man walked out of the store with a white bag containing a soup and sandwich. He stopped and looked at me and said, "Thank you so much, Mister." He walked away from the scene with his dignity intact. I watched him cross the street and nestle into a corner in an alley between two buildings where he sat on a collapsed shipping box and slowly ate a large sandwich with a hot bowl of soup. I bet he was savoring every bite. It felt so good knowing that I helped a hungry man, even if it was only for a few hours. I had fulfilled my duty to him. It was the least I could do.

Why was it worth it to me to buy the man lunch when nobody around me would? Well, yes, you guessed it: I acted out of positive and negative reinforcement viewed through the prism of my genetics and historical context. It was more rewarding and valuable for me to buy the man a seven dollar lunch than it was for me to let the man walk away hungry. I was negatively reinforced by removing the awful feeling of saying no and watching a fellow man walk away hungry, with all of the benefit of life I had. By giving, I was taking away a negative stimulus—the feeling of guilt and shame—from my own body. I was also positively reinforced by the intrinsic value I received for helping the man. It feels good to help people who are poor and less fortunate.

There was also a historical social context, as I hated to know that someone was hungry in a food-plentiful environment. I was taught to feed those who are hungry when there is food available. I value diminishing hunger in those around me if I am able to do so. This is a point of honor and hospitality in my ancestral culture. As I was reared in a traditional Lebanese household, it is part of our culture to be hospitable to company around us, especially when it comes to food and drink. So, it was highly valuable to me for that man not to leave the scene in hunger. My historical context was playing a strong role in this situation.

It would have picked at me had I let him walk away hungry. Why was it me and not anyone else on the patio, to help feed that hungry man? It was because it was worth more to me than it was to the other patio dwellers. I was chasing perceived value. I got the value that I so craved at that moment by acting as I did. It was a silent contract executed to the letter. I get what I want and the homeless man gets what he wants. *Quid pro quo* (something for something). The universal law of all relationships. Had my brother been sitting there, he would have probably done the same thing.

We have very similar genes and were reared in very similar environments. The values of my brothers and I are quite parallel. Right after I told him this story, my dentist brother actually told me that he bought a poor Mexican family a meal in a restaurant in California. He paid the bill and left without them knowing. He told the man working the restaurant not to bring them the food until he was gone. My brother had seen two young kids and an apparently poor mother and father sharing a single meal. Like me, he was compelled to act.

Similarly, it was a big deal to me to help that man relative to anyone on that patio that day, all else being equal. The perceived value the people thought they would receive from buying the man lunch was less than seven dollars and the time it took to accommodate him. In other words, the cost of the situation was seven dollars and a little time and energy. That was too costly for the onlookers, but to me there was more benefit in it than a handful of change and a little hassle to know that a hungry man could walk away with a wholesome meal and a little dignity. That is why I was the only one who acted. I know it sounds a little mechanical and economical, but it can't be explained any other way.

I was asked, "What if people are just nice and act out of their hearts?" I was nice and acted out of my heart. That doesn't mean I don't attribute some value to it or know there are costs involved. It is our duty, as humans, to assist the less fortunate when we are able to do so. Failing to assist those who are poor and in need, when we are able to help, is the apex of human ignorance. Giving to those in need legitimizes our own possessions.

CHAPTER 14 - The Troubled

The greatest asset a book like this can give you is the ability to properly observe, understand, and to some degree predict human behavior, and that has real value in all walks of life and all occupations. Behavioral manipulation has been used as long as humans have been conscious of themselves as thinking and acting beings. The word 'manipulation' in the behavioral sense need not always carry a negative connotation. At times, behavioral manipulation, alteration, and modification can be a life-saver to someone involved in an out-of-control, self-destructive behavior such as alcoholism, gambling, or anorexia.

Think about what you do that you know is not good for you. Could you do it less? Could you stop doing it? If not, why? Ask yourself. What is the method of your madness? Why do you continue to do that? Whatever it is, you are going to do it to a lesser degree, as well as step back and ponder your strength and knowledge about the propellers of your behavior. Because we know behavior to be lawful, we can use the laws that govern behavior to manipulate human behavior for the betterment of individuals, and to a larger extent, society as a whole. I hope to start with just one person and make the world a better place, bit by bit. Just as we use the laws of math to build bridges, we can use the laws of human psychology and behavior to help build personal bridges to better places. We will make valiant attempts to engineer pathways and processes to alter behavior for the betterment of all.

The number of people with harmful drug addictions of all types, and those with catastrophic, debilitating disorders such as anorexia, bulimia, phobias, anxiety, panic attacks, obsessions, compulsions, and many other psychopathologies, is staggering. Understanding *why* we do what we do via the predictable principles of behavior, whilst highlighting one's genetics and context, will allow us to uncover behavioral antidotes. In this way the self-destructive actor can be helped. Some may not be cured but at least they can be managed. With this in mind, let me offer you a true story, and just another example of why we need to intervene and help those who need assistance. Such intervention and help will allow them to better cope and deal with the world in a more beneficial way for themselves and their loved ones. The world can be a cold place at times, and I hope that by seeing it for what it is, we can all help to warm it up a little.

Several years ago, a longtime friend of mine—let's call him 'Joe'—began to use crack cocaine, and he quickly found himself in a downward spiral. It was July of 2007. I hadn't seen my friend in weeks, and no one knew his whereabouts. We lived in the mini-Saudi Arabia—'Oil Country'—a province otherwise known as Alberta in Canada. This created a rapid influx of young blue collar males from all over the country coming here and seeking well-paying jobs. The city was booming in all aspects: infrastructure, real estate, small business, etc. There was money growing on trees. Unfortunately, this was also at a time when the drug business was flourishing in the city of Edmonton. Even low level street dealers were offered incentive packages to work a phone and be a 'dial-a-doper', delivering drugs. Some of the incentives included a free car, a cell phone, a place to stay and bail money if they got busted dealing, ensuring they would keep their mouths shut with the cops. These enterprises operated no differently than your typical small business. All types of businesses were flourishing no matter what their legitimacy. Working as a lawyer, I couldn't believe just how many people were in the "game" (the drug business). A 17 year-old going nowhere fast could be at a fork in the road in his young life. His choices could be to work at McDonalds for $12 an hour or to become a dial-a-doper and make $1000 a day, with all the perks included. For many who had little guidance, the latter, not the former, would be their choice. This just served to perpetuate the game.

Two friends and I were driving in the downtown core one night when we received a phone call from someone we knew, tipping us off that he had seen our dear lost friend at a certain place about a 10-minute drive from where we were. My friends and I drove to the location where our troubled friend was spotted. Our source pulled up and said, "He was just here a minute ago. He was sitting with those guys." He pointed to a stoop at the side of a building in a shady part of the city notorious for crime and drugs. There were three people sitting on the stoop.

The younger male with the couple had messy hair and clothes that were dirty. His eyes were bloodshot, he looked malnourished, and he couldn't sit still. He kept getting off the stoop and walking around like he was looking for something. He was probably just growing crazily impatient as he waited for his next hit. He was part of the drug underworld, and we were in the heart of it.

He looked at us with contempt. My friend in the passenger seat announced, "Hey, we're looking for Joe. Have you seen him?"

They all looked at us dumbly, as they were skeptical about giving information to us since we were unknown figures. We could have been any number of people in their eyes, from drug dealers to undercover cops to debt collectors. We knew they knew whom we were asking for, yet the Caucasian man looked my friend square in the face and said, "I don't know who you're talking about." We knew that he was lying. He knew exactly who we were looking for. My friend in the passenger seat got hot under the collar and said, "Hey, we're not cops, we're thugs! Now, where the hell is he?"

The skinny man muttered, "Hey guys, I don't know anything," as he mischievously smirked at us and walked backwards toward where the couple was sitting quietly.

As all this was taking place, our source had spotted our troubled friend down the block walking with a few "acquaintances." Just then, two city policemen pulled up in a cruiser. They were a little suspicious of us in this place, possibly thinking we could be dealers. They jumped out of their vehicle, and the driver walked up and asked, "What are you guys doing here?"

We explained that we were looking for our friend who was caught up in this mess and needed help. The cop said, "You guys must be looking for Joe. I almost arrested him today."

I said, "Yeah, that's him," and we all got out of our Ford Explorer.

My two friends went with the source to find our troubled friend— now spotted just a block away—while I stayed and talked to the policemen. The same cop asked me, "So what do you do?"

I jumped. "Hey, don't get the wrong idea!" I said. "I practice law, and we are here to rescue our friend from this hellhole."

Whyology

The cop commended me for coming down to rescue our friend from a neighborhood of crime, hunger, desperation, and drug use. I distinctly remember the cop looking at me closely and saying in a reduced tone, "If you don't get your friend out of here, he will become a shell of a man just like all the others out here." I smelled aromas of garbage and sewage hanging in the humid air from the back alley, and my hair stood up sharply on the back of my neck as the cop uttered those unforgettable words to me.

"I think they found him, and we're taking him home," I asserted to the cop. I waited on the side of the building with the policemen for the other guys to come back with our troubled friend. They didn't show up. Finally, the cop said, "Get into the back of my car—let's go for a ride and find these guys."

I opened the back door of the police car and got in, feeling like a criminal blocked off by the glass barrier dividing me and the two cops in the front seat. The door latches were removed from the inside, and the back of the car smelled like metal and body odor. We drove around the area looking for the guys. No luck. The cop sped up and down alleyways and streets, cursing. "Where the hell are these guys?"

Out of luck, we went back to where the Explorer was parked, and they suddenly emerged from the alley: our lost friend was found. The cop stopped the car and opened my door from the outside, as there was no way for me to get out alone. "Get this guy out of here," demanded the cop.

I couldn't believe my eyes. Our dear friend had lost about 30 of his 230 pounds. His face was dirty, and his hair was matted, and he had a beard. His fingers were burnt and rough from using crack, as it is smoked through all sorts of metal and glass contraptions that are not always finger-friendly when a flame gets involved. His eyes were sunken in, and his teeth were stained from smoking cigarettes and other substances.

We got into the Explorer, and our troubled friend sat next to me in the back. He gazed at me across the seat, speechless. He looked like he was coming off a recent hit of crack, as his eyes were unfocused and he seemed agitated. It hurt us to see our lifelong friend like this. He looked guilty, impatient, inattentive, aloof, relieved, and frustrated—all at the same time. He needed detox really badly: he told us that he hadn't slept for the last three days, and that he was almost stabbed in some basement the night

141

before. He wasn't eating or sleeping well. I barely recognized our dear friend when he emerged from the shadows of the alleyway. He sat in the vehicle staring into space, his mind racing, not thinking his friends would be sitting in front of him at that moment in time. He was in too deep to feel shame, or anything for that matter. He wondered, more to himself, "What the hell are you guys doing here?" a few times. He hadn't showered in a while and his clothes and body absolutely reeked.

He was visibly pissed off at us for driving him out of the area against our promises not to take him away. The area was littered with pawnshops, prostitutes, needles, bums, junkies, and condoms, and sporadically patrolled by cops. The cop had described the area as "hell on earth" as his beat festered with misery, hunger, despair, hopelessness and helplessness. The majority of the city was full of great communities with friendly and warm people. However, like any big city with a booming economy, it had its share of problem areas. This was one of them. It was where misery could find company. This is where our dear friend wanted to be. He threatened to take his shoes off if we didn't stop the SUV. We kept driving against his constant cries for us to stop. He took his shoes off and grinned at me. He put one of his feet onto the middle console between the two front seats that my friends were sitting in. The smell that came from those socks and those shoes was the most putrid stench I'd ever breathed in. We instantly covered our faces and pleaded with him to put his shoes back on. His feet were raw from walking for hours on end in the intense summer heat. He was very irritable, and didn't want to leave the area. We had to lie to him and defy his wishes at all costs. Lying had real value here: it was in his best interests to leave the area, even if he didn't think it was. We didn't know what to do with him, but he was coming by force. One idea we had was to take him to a field by our houses and call up a few of the boys to kick the shit out of him. A good dose of tough love was what came to mind. That wouldn't really solve the problem, though it might help temporarily.

I had known my troubled friend for 25 years. It was a terrible thing to see, but it was as raw and real as life gets. He had no room for superficial niceties: all was bent toward the chase to get that next hit. Family, friends, health, well-being, integrity, and honesty were worthless. All that mattered was the vice. It hurt me deeply to see my friend at such a low. I couldn't help trying to get inside his troubled mind. *Why is he doing this?* I silently asked myself as the four of us drove toward home, away from that neighborhood. It was a mosaic of madness, in a place that overtook and heightened the senses. You could see it, smell it, hear it, taste it and feel it, before it began to leave you deadened and empty. It truly engulfed the senses being in an area of town like that. I couldn't help thinking hard about what to do with this troubled person from a psychological point of view. This guy became the most important case I had encountered to date. What could I do to make my friend discontinue this systematic mode of self-destruction? I tried to make sense of it because all behavior made sense. Once again, it's all lawful.

When we were driving in the Explorer with my troubled friend, he demanded of us, "Why don't you guys mind your own business? Why should I stop doing this shit?" Nobody said anything until I looked at him and said directly, "You should stop doing this because you're hurting yourself and others who care about you." He looked at me with contempt because he knew I was the educated and rational one in the vehicle, and he didn't say another word. I had to hit him hard with a shot of reality. I carried on and shouted, "You think we want to see you doing this shit and ruining your life?" He still didn't respond, becoming more agitated by my words. He knew I was being straight up and as true as can be. When I am furious with someone, my words can be deadly sharp, but sometimes that's what people need.

Behavior is reinforced in a biopsychosocial world, meaning that we give things value via biological, psychological and social avenues. It is up to the psychologist to attempt to undo certain parts of these connections in the destructive behavioral cycle and replace them with other forms of value that have an overshadowing importance in the actor's mind. This is a slow and delicate process when we deal with someone like a crack user or a person who does other drugs. The value these people attain when they commit such behaviors is so great that finding a combination of biopsychosocial valuables to act as a counterweight to the reinforcing harmful behavior is a great challenge, although still very possible.

One of the largest problems when it comes to patterns of addiction is context or environment. That is the primary reason for taking a person out of the environment where they frequently commit destructive behaviors, and this separation is sometimes half of the battle. My friend's value structure in that context was out of whack, and he needed to get help to have it altered.

Our value structures change with context to a certain degree. My troubled friend moved far away to escape the multitude of triggers in his drug abusing context. The variables of context in the behavioral equation were changed when my friend left town. A change of context is one of the best starts to the path of recovery because the antecedent variables leading to the destructive behavior are changed or lost. Due to the fact that our genetic portion of the behavioral equation never changes we must go after the environmental side and attack context, beliefs and perceptions, whilst educating the troubled subject. Leaving this context gave my friend the push he needed to begin changing his life. He dug deep, and he beat it. Context always matters, as do genes.

Certain things such as drugs and gambling, will be more rewarding to one person as opposed to another simply because of the genetic codes inherited from biological parents. Thinking about trying crack? Don't ever even try it once. For many, all it takes is just one hit, and you're done. Crystal meth works in the same way, except it is cheaper, lasts longer, and is more destructive to the user's health. My friend liked crack just as I love sunflower seeds: it jived with him. It served a purpose, because as I stated earlier, all behavior is purposive. Why is it that you can have two brothers reared in the same home, and one could absolutely love smoking marijuana, and the other can't even tolerate the smell of it? The simple answer is genetic predisposition. That is one part of the equation, and it can't be altered. On the flip side, that's also the reason why addiction patterns tend to run in families. Context is the other part of the equation.

I hate it when people say that when someone has an addiction to something like alcohol it is a "disease." It is in no way a disease. That is the biggest cop out I have ever heard. It is just that certain people have strong genetic predispositions (along with cultural pressures) to using and enjoying alcohol, and because of that, they will more likely become addicted to it. Environment matters as well. If an alcoholic was raised from birth in a country like Saudi Arabia where consumption of alcohol is illegal, would he have this "disease" at the same point in time in his life? A disease is something that someone contracts that is purely unwanted and unwelcome. Couldn't we then point to a criminal and say that he committed the crime because he has a disease, he really needed to do what he did, and therefore he is not responsible? To say that is to say he is not in control but that the disease is in control. This dilutes the moral blameworthiness for their actions. Sure certain genetic propensities tend to make people act in one

144

way as opposed to another, but we are all responsible for what we do even if we have been dealt a disadvantageous genetic hand.

There are, however, instances where people truly are ill and have mental issues that make them do certain things while not appreciating that their actions are wrong. This is a grey area that will find itself in court rooms until the end of time. While I believe that genetic precursors have an effect on our actions, attributing action to them is a virtually impossible connection to make and hence they have little effect on punishments. Barring real psychopathologies, such as paranoid schizophrenia or delusional disorders, we must be held accountable for our actions and garner the will to fight our harmful acts. Sometimes this can only be done with the assistance of a mental health practitioner coupled with a change in environment.

I aim to assist those such as my troubled friend to show onlookers that recovery is possible by using the laws of human behavior. The tool box of basic principles of human psychology and reinforcement, along with an in depth understanding of an individual's historical and current context and genetics, makes it possible to achieve such a feat. Part of the reason I wrote this book was in an attempt to band-aid the ills of mankind and stop the heartache of millions who live with addictions and other behavioral problems destroying both themselves and those they love. Behavioral manipulation, through understanding what propels our behavior via the principles of biobehaviorism, will assist people in conquering their demons. Each patient/case is different, and values vary from person to person. Accordingly, each behavioral treatment regime should be tailored to suit the needs of the patient. This treatment should be based on the underlying reinforcement mechanisms and genetic markers or predispositions at play in that patient. Our value systems and hierarchies are purely unique and exclusive from all others. It is the uncovering and understanding of the mechanisms of value and reinforcement that will assist you in starting on your path of change.

The more we understand the basic principles of the lawfulness of behavior, the easier it will be for us to manipulate certain harmful behaviors and alter our destructive patterns. The principles of biobehaviorism are especially effective in manipulating the behavior and value structures in a way that alters what we perceive to be valuable. In order to do that, we must have things of value that we perceive as greater than the value derived from drugs or other dangers. The problem with crack cocaine in particular, is that it is such a reinforcing drug that finding a counterweight to the reinforcement value garnered by it is almost impossible. That is why millions of people remain hooked on the drug. Crack is basically powder cocaine mixed with baking soda and cooked so that it turns into a beige crystalline lump that looks like candle wax. It is smoked in its solid form, and it takes just seven seconds from the time it is smoked until the time it hits the bloodstream, bringing a rush of euphoria. It is an extremely good and quick high (no, I've never, ever tried it). It's the great escape, condensed into a few grains in the palm of your hand. This escape and feeling of euphoria have strong reinforcing value for the user, meaning that what the drug does and how it makes the user feel will make it more likely that the user will indulge in it again in the future.

Remember, something is a reinforcer if it makes the behaviors leading up to it more likely to occur in the future. However, serious drug use almost always comes at the expense of other things, and sometimes those 'things' are people who care about you. With continued substance abuse, or acted-out destructive behaviors, it is inevitable that we break the hearts of those closest to us. Victims become scattered everywhere: mothers, fathers, siblings, and friends.

Intervention works on the counterweight principle because it has sufficiently strong value to the self-destructive actor to compete with their addiction or vice. Intervention brings all of the meaningful people in one's life together to tell the addict how they feel, how they are affected, and why they want the person to stop using. On the one side of the scale are the drugs and their effects, and on the other side of the scale is everyone important in that person's life. This method places the implicit cost-benefit analysis of the addict in a revealing light: there is so much at stake against the drugs that it becomes the heaviest counterweight to assist in cessation of drug use. All of the people out there who care about you, giving you an ultimatum, and forcing you to take responsibility, offers one of the strongest possible counterweights to an out-of-control addictive behavior.

The more people who come forward and plead together with an addicted person, the more valuable it becomes for that person to stop using. Couple that with education, an immediate change in context and a genuine desire for the user to stop, and we are on the right track to recovery. Enough people can serve as a pocket of value to outweigh the value received by the use of the drugs. Many take heed that they will lose it all if they don't make a valiant attempt to change their ways. As stated, this is a delicate process and proper steps are needed at the outset, or it will be too much of a shock for the addict to think about losing such a reinforcing vice. This graduated process must involve a large counterweight with unconditional support that is stern and unwavering, acting against the destructive behavioral pattern. It's like my gambler friend who quit because of the new love in his life. She was a substantial enough counterweight to compete with the value he derived from gambling. If the pattern of behavior is highly destructive to the user (such as a crack addiction) then a change of context, possibly to a treatment facility is the next best course of action.

Taking an addicted person out of his or her context bolsters the chance of success as he or she will not be in an environment rich with precursors to use, such as home life, peer pressures, stress and other things that facilitate and act as a catalyst for drug use or other harmful behavior. These are called the antecedents of behavior, and as they change so too does our behavior. We can't change our genes, but we can change what stimuli our genes interact with and understand the push and pull of why we do what we do.

The misery festering in people all around us hits home time and time again when I get stray phone calls at my office asking what can be done about a drug abusing son who is out of control. I go from lawyer to psychologist in seconds. It's in me to give, and it would be absurd to not give what advice I could to a desperate parent on the other end of the line. The beauty of my unique situation is that I've seen the potential heights of knowledge and understanding in academia, and I've seen the worst depths of the streets. I have a very balanced perspective of the world, in legitimate and illegitimate guises. I have an in-depth understanding of both sides of the coin and can understand people at all levels. I can converse with a judge, a detective, a bum, a drug dealer, a thug, and an addict with similar proficiency and with the right lingo. I'm as much street smart as I am book smart, and that's what allows me to see the world as I do, coupled with my in-depth knowledge of psychology. What good would this knowledge be if it were locked up in my head until I took it to my grave? I strongly believe that special knowledge must be shared with humanity so that we can collectively evolve in a positive direction among the many negatives in the world.

Some of the psychology courses I enrolled in were centered on behavioral modification and therapy. If we knew the *"why"* about behavior, we could alter certain variables in the equation to bring about a new result, using different modes of behavioral therapy from the laws of behavior. With this in mind, I feel it is my duty to stop the heartache of so many, and it is the duty of the rest of you who read this book to work at improving your world and the world of those close to you. This can only be achieved through observation, understanding, prediction and modification of our behaviors for the betterment of all. While certain harmful acts we engage in will always bring us perceived value, if we can't quit them, *we must at the very least manage them.*

CHAPTER 15 - Catch Yourself

As continual value seekers, we continue to look to the future and reminisce about the past relative to what we have experienced in our lives up until the present moment. With so much value-chasing going on, this ultimately leads to stresses and bouts of suffering at one junction or another. The stresses or suffering may be generalized and chronic, or they may emerge, sudden and acute. Whatever the cause, severity or frequency, there must be a way to escape from the crush of the value chase using the same principles of behavior that drive the pursuit.

As I said earlier, we live our lives in a whirlwind of fear and hope, which affects the way we react to the things that make up our environments. We fear uncertainty; we fear what has made us scared in the past or what we think we might encounter in the future. Many of our thoughts are negative. We have numerous expectations to live up to in a multitude of areas in our lives. When we fail or when we don't live up to our expectations, stress and suffering will catch up with us. This just adds to the already hectic lives we have to deal with. *Why* continue to suffer or be stressed?

In order to decompress and feel some inner peace, we must learn to detach ourselves from chasing things of value to us. This doesn't mean abandoning your values; it means stopping for a moment and reflecting on what it is that is making you suffer, because we all suffer.

Suffering is almost always related to value lost or unattained which may be compounded by a skewed perception of what is real and what isn't through our system of beliefs. What kind of value have you perceived to have lost or missed that is making you suffer? It must be something. It has to be. Once you know the answer to that, you can start the process toward feeling better and to managing and curtailing your stress. Only then can you truly decompress and find that hidden sanctuary within you.

Just *be*, letting all that you perceive as having an iota of value become meaningless. At least once a day (I recommend), we must stop for a moment and get to a place or state within ourselves where we seek no value: nothing in our actions or our thoughts, no thoughts about the past or the future! All we should care about is achieving an inner peacefulness that is disconnected from anything we perceive to have value. We must detach in order to decompress. We must detach from value lost, possessed, or unattained. That is why people feel so good when they come back from vacation after working for a long time. They have detached, decompressed, and exposed their senses to novel stimuli.

Detachment is one of the best ways to achieve the point of inner peace that we should get to at least once a day. If you're really stressed or suffering, you should seek that place more often or for longer periods. As we sit still, devoid of any stimulation, we must try to concentrate as we would do when meditating. We must come to a conclusion within ourselves that all material objects have no value. Money has no value either. All of your possessions, no matter how much they cost in the real world, have no value in this state. All you should be concerned with in the zero value state is being cognizant and conscious with your mind as a blank slate. The present environment has no significance, and you are detached from all that you concern yourself with or stress and suffer over.

One of the reasons that many of us are stressed is that when it comes to past or future events, we tend to think in a pattern referred to as serial thinking. We start with one thought, and that thought leads to another, and another, and so on. Serial thinking is one of the most dangerous thought patterns that we have the capacity and potential to engage in. Our thoughts become littered with *what if*, and *if only I didn't*, and so on until we drive ourselves mad. This is very unhealthy. Catch yourself and stop yourself before you sink deeper into that mental abyss of tangled thoughts. Become conscious of your thoughts, but don't allow them to consume your consciousness. These series of connected thoughts that cause us stress, because of fear based on our past experiences (or thoughts of the future), are toxic to our well-being. We might think of a particular negative future event, followed by another, and so on until our thoughts are out of control. It is a continuous mental imaging and ballooning mental pattern of what happened or will happen.

Since many of our thoughts are negative, we must take time to clear our minds from this mental junk every so often, just to feel grounded and positive. As highly sophisticated entities atop the animal kingdom, we are more complex than we ourselves can appreciate. With so much information flowing into our conscious and unconscious minds, there is a plethora of mental information that will undoubtedly bring us stress when we begin to think about it. That being said, we must clear our minds of all value (past, present and future) and just *be*, if only for a few moments.

To achieve peacefulness, you must strive to become a blank slate, with your mind as clear as possible. Once you realize that you can do this, you will be amazed at the feeling that you get. Your stress will inevitably be reduced and you will ultimately suffer less. Life is too short to constantly be bogged down with anxiety, stress, and suffering. Sit still and try to attain that zero value state. It's not hard: take some good breaths and decompress as you attempt to reach that state. All that matters is the vessel holding your mind. You seek neither to reduce tension nor to add value. Your simple goal is to detach from all you think and value and to just become in tune with your vessel. Just *be*. Don't think, don't care, don't talk, don't wonder, don't hope—just be still. All has no value.

A zero value state is the only state in which we can truly be at peace with ourselves. Zero value states not only ground you, but they add some balance and humility to your life. Remember, balance is very important. Even though you stand at the center of your selfish pursuits and are always chasing value, it's unhealthy to be in that constant mental state of value-chasing all of the time. Because we must eat, drink, and sleep—and do all of the vices and pastimes that consume us—we can't be in a zero value state for a long time. We are deferred by the stereotypical behavioral patterns tied to our core needs. They are physiologically driven. These behaviors are distinct from all other behaviors in that they are necessity-driven as opposed to want-driven. Nonetheless, for a brief moment of total mental control, these basic human needs play no role in a true zero value state. You can achieve value by giving value to nothing, in order to be at one with yourself and detach from all you perceive as valuable.

Recharged, you must get on with the business of life, meaning the business of value-chasing. It is what you do. Some value chasing is needed for survival and some just to satisfy our wants. Nonetheless, it is what it is. You do what you do, because it's all about you. Don't be ashamed that you're selfish; we all are. To be selfish is to be human and to be human is to be selfish. Just give something back to make you and your possessions a legitimate part of the world you work in.

Whyology

Now that you are familiar with some concepts and laws of psychology, I want you to take away a few things from this work. Firstly, even though it's all about you (us), we must be amenable to the interests of others, as long as those interests don't trample too hard on our own. We must be tolerant of others and step into the shoes of those that are different than us. We must refrain from being judgmental, because all behavior has an explanation. Instead of judging, we must ask why and understand through the lens of biobehaviorism. We must live and let live to the greatest extent possible. Only a portion of our behavior is governed by what we have learned. A large part of how we behave is fixed by our genetic inheritance that makes us part of who we are, prior to any environmental exposure. Thus, give deference to genetically-driven vices or psychopathologies.

I inherited some unwanted traits from my parents that afflict me, irrespective of the environment I was to grow up in. No matter where on earth I was placed from birth, I would suffer from these genetically fixed mental plagues. These inherited problems are part of the realm of my geneavior and are present completely exclusive of environmental inputs. What personality disorder or inherited flaw did you inherit from your parents? Was it anxiety? Or was it something else? Was it depression? Was it something worse? Whatever it is, we all have these fixed psychological and biological patterns within us simply because of genetic inheritance. Psychological and biological disorders afflict many people. They didn't choose these afflictions; their genetics did. Thus, let's be more tolerant of those around us and understand through the principles of biobehaviorism why it is someone did or said something.

Using the laws of psychology, we can assist those who are in real need of change from their destructive behavioral patterns. The goal is to redirect value from what the destructive person seeks to attain. We must educate and alter the behaviors of those who are in need of change. Through behavioral modification, therapy—and, as a last resort, medication—we will attempt to steer those who chase destructive value toward value-chasing behaviors that are safe and progressive.

The first step toward real change is an in-depth interview with a psychologist or a sincere conversation with someone close to you followed by human support, facing the problem head-on. Allowing yourself to acknowledge there is a problem and a desire to change is paramount. After this, a contextual change may be necessary in those instances where the problem is relatively harmful and the context itself may be assisting in making the harmful behaviors more likely to occur. We all must regain control and free ourselves and others from our destructive patterns of behavior.

Catch yourself. Think about what you are doing and why. Let's stop the heartache of all the poor mothers, fathers, children, and siblings out there who endure so much pain at the hands of their kin who continue on a path of destructive value-chasing. Those of you who have really learned what the building blocks of behavior are will begin on the glorious new path by altering harmful behavioral patterns so as to make your lives change for the better. In order to change our behaviors, we must redirect them from what we currently value. It's all about value.

The purpose of this book is to educate all who read it in the ways all humans behave on a moment-to-moment basis and the motivations behind those actions. I hope that you have read between the lines and you are truly seeing the behavior of yourself and others for what they really are. Due to the assertion that we are vessels of free will, we will be held accountable for all of our actions, notwithstanding the fact that we may be able to point to strong genetic predispositions as the culprit that led to the trend toward certain behaviors.

This book is more a self-understanding book then it is a self-help book; to help thy self, you must first understand thy self. Not only is this book meant to help those who are afflicted by harmful behavioral patterns, but it is a helpful tool for those in the disciplines of law, engineering, social work, counseling, psychology, rehabilitation, commerce, personal relations, politics, business, advertising, marketing, architecture, etc. and, most importantly, life in general. It assists in predicting behavior, which is very important in all walks of life. I really hope that you see the world a little more clearly and that you are a little less ignorant when it comes to the *why* behind the way someone has behaved.

ALL behavior has explanation, no matter what, and all human behaviors are self-interested. It can always be broken down into the **WHY**. What are *your* interests? Ask yourself now! What are they? What do you value? Why do you do what you do, and what are you going to do next? I hope you now know **why**, because there is always a why. It's simply *whyology*.

NOTES

Notes to Chapter 2:
[1] Hobbes, T. (2010) A.P. Martinich & B. Battiste (Eds.) *Leviathan*. Peterborough, ON:
     Broadview, 123.
[2] Hobbes, 128.
[3] Bartol, C.R. (1995) *Criminal Behavior: A Psychosocial Approach*. (4th ed.) Englewood Cliffs, NJ: Prentice Hall, 140.
[4] Ariely, D. (2009) *Predictably Irrational*. (Rev ed.) New York, NY: Harper Perennial.

Notes to Chapter 3:
[1] Freud, S. (1962) J. Strachey. (Ed.) J. Riviere (Trans.) *The Ego and the Id*. London:
     Hogarth Press and Institute of Psychoanalysis, 15.
[2] Hall, C.S., Lindzey, G & Campbell, J.B. (1998) *Theories of Personality*. (4th ed.) New York, NY: John Wiley & Sons, 77.
[3] Skinner, B.F. (1974) *About Behaviorism*. New York, NY: Alfred A. Knopf.
[4] Hall et al., 505.
[5] Hall et al., 505.
[6] Hall et al., 498.
[7] Breland, K. & Breland, M. (1961) The Misbehavior of Organisms. *American Psychologist* 16, 681-684.
[8] Domjan, M. (1998) *The Principles of Learning and Behavior*. (4th ed.) Pacific Grove, CA: Brooks/Cole Publishing Company, 140.
[9] Lipsitt, L.P. (2002, March) Minds don't snap. Op-Ed. Retrieved from:
     http://brown.edu/Administration/News_Bureau/2001-02/01-100.html n.p.
[10] Lipsitt, n.p.

Notes to Chapter 5:
[1] Locke, J. (1690) *An Essay Concerning Human Understanding*.

Notes to Chapter 7:
[1] See, for example, Lennon, S.J. & Davis, L.L. (1989) Categorization in first impressions. *Journal of Psychology: Interdisciplinary and Applied*, 123(5), 439-446, and Davis, L.L. & Lennon, S.J. (1988) Social cognition and the study of clothing and human behavior. *Social Behavior and Personality*, 16(2), 175-186.

Notes to Chapter 8:
[1] Byrne, R. (2006) *The Secret*. Hillsboro, OR: Beyond Words Publishing.
[2] Byrne, R. & Harrington, P. (Producers) (2006) *The Secret*. [Motion Picture] United States: Prime Time Productions.

Notes to Chapter 9:
[1] Pavlov, I.P. (1927) *Conditional Reflexes*. New York, NY: Dover Publications.
[2] Sutton, J.G. (2008), Jan. 30) Inspiration v. Perspiration. Article. Retrieved from: http://www.psychicworld.net/InspiredWriting.htm. n.p.
[3] Sutton, n.p.

Notes to Chapter 10:
[1] Domjan, 143.

Notes to Chapter 11:
[1] Harris, J.R. (2006) *No Two Alike*. New York, NY: W.W. Norton & Company.
[2] Harris.
[3] Harris, 2.

Notes to Chapter 13:
[1] Darley, J.M. & Latané, B. (1968) Bystander intervention in emergencies: diffusion of responsibility, *Journal of Personality and Social Psychology*, 8, 377-383.
[2] Milgram, S. (1970) The experience of living in cities. *Science*, 167, 1461-1468.

Made in the USA
Lexington, KY
15 February 2013